COOKING FOR SPECIAL OCCASIONS

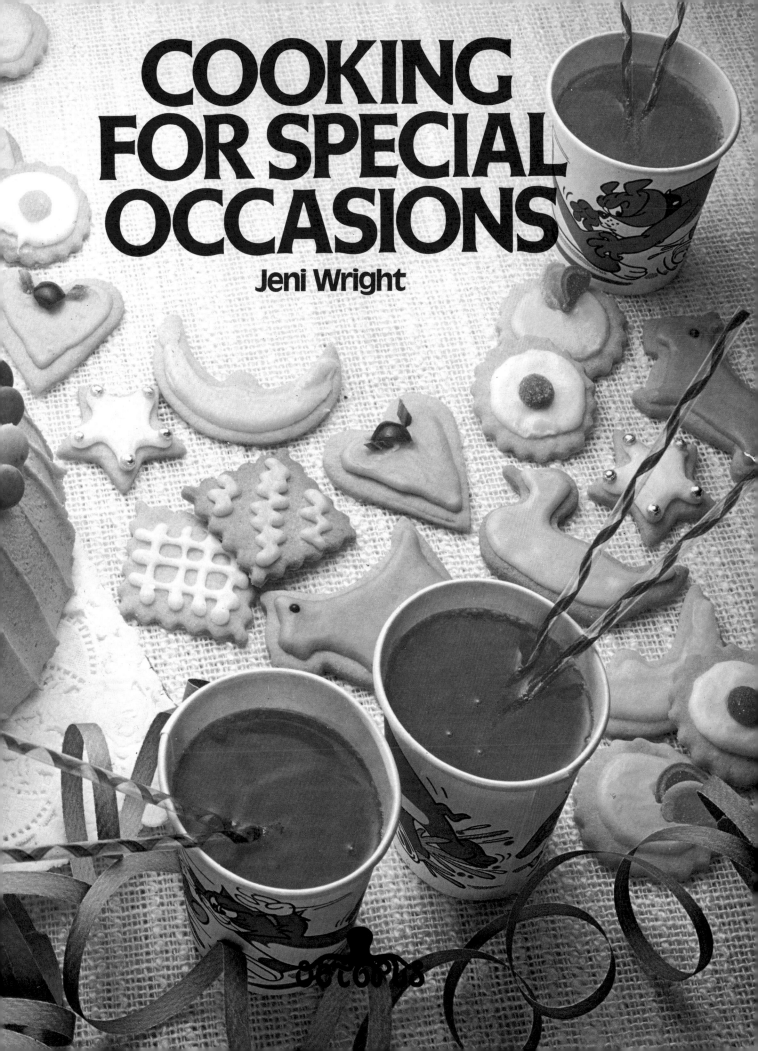

COOKING FOR SPECIAL OCCASIONS

Jeni Wright

octopus

Contents

This edition first published in 1978 by
Octopus Books Limited
59 Grosvenor Street, London W1

© 1977 Hennerwood Publications Limited

ISBN 0 7064 0775 X

Produced by Mandarin Publishers Limited,
22a Westlands Road, Quarry Bay, Hong Kong

Printed in Hong Kong

Gone are the days when a wine and cheese party meant cubes of pineapple and cheese on sticks and a few bottles of cheap wine. A party with a theme such as this gives the host or hostess plenty of scope to be imaginative, particularly with the immense variety of American and imported cheeses that are available.

In addition to the dishes you choose to cook for the party, you will also want to offer your guests a good cheeseboard. When choosing cheeses for this make sure that your selection includes both hard and soft, and blue cheeses, as well as a number of the more unusual and attractive kinds such as the French cheeses that are covered in grape seeds or halved walnuts. Goat's cheese comes in a variety of shapes and sizes – and is also quite different in flavor from cheese made with cow's milk – therefore these would add interest. Arrange different colors and textures together to make an eye-catching board, and serve with a selection of unusual crackers and crispbreads, as well as French and wholewheat breads. Bowls of crisp, fresh fruit add color and also complement the texture of cheese. Most of the recipes serve between ten and fifteen people as part of a buffet party spread.

Spinach and cheese quiche

For the pastry:
$\frac{3}{4}$ cup all-purpose flour
Pinch of salt
$\frac{3}{4}$ cup wholewheat flour
$\frac{1}{4}$ lb (1 stick) butter or margarine
About $\frac{1}{4}$ cup cold water to mix

For the filling:
$1\frac{1}{2}$ cups cottage cheese, forced through a strainer
1 whole egg, beaten
3 egg yolks, beaten
$\frac{2}{3}$ cup sour cream
$\frac{1}{2}$ teaspoon grated nutmeg
Salt and freshly ground black pepper
3 packages frozen chopped spinach, thawed
$\frac{1}{2}$ cup grated Cheddar cheese
$\frac{1}{2}$ teaspoon cayenne

Cooking Time: 50 minutes.
Oven: 400°F.

To make the pastry: sift the all-purpose flour and salt into a mixing bowl. Stir in the wholewheat flour. Add the butter or margarine in pieces and rub into the flour until the mixture resembles fine breadcrumbs. Stir in enough cold water to hold the mixture together. Form into a ball, wrap in foil or wax paper and chill in the refrigerator for at least 30 minutes before using.

Roll out the dough on a floured board and use to line an 11 inch quiche pan or ring, placed on a baking sheet. Prick the base with a fork. Line the dough with foil, fill with dry beans and bake blind in a fairly hot oven for 10 minutes, then remove beans and foil and continue baking for another 5 minutes. Remove from oven and set aside.

To prepare filling: put the cottage cheese, eggs and sour cream in a bowl and mix well. Stir in half the nutmeg and salt and pepper to taste. Put the spinach in the base of the pastry case, sprinkle with salt and pepper and the remaining nutmeg, then pour over the cottage cheese mixture. Mix the grated Cheddar cheese with the cayenne and sprinkle over the quiche.

Bake in a fairly hot oven for approximately 35 minutes until the filling is set and the cheese topping is golden. Remove from the oven and serve warm, cut into wedges. Cuts into 16 wedges.

Swiss cheese fondue; Spinach and cheese quiche

Swiss cheese fondue

1 garlic clove, peeled and cut in half
2½ cups dry white wine
2 teaspoons lemon juice
1 lb Swiss cheese, grated
1 lb Cheddar cheese, grated
2 tablespoons cornstarch
¼ cup Kirsch
Pinch of cayenne
Freshly ground black pepper
1–2 long loaves French bread cut into 1 in cubes

Remember to tell your guests the old Swiss saying that if one of the gentlemen guests drops his cube of bread in the fondue pot, then he must buy the next bottle of wine; if a lady drops her cube of bread, then she must kiss all the men present. Traditionally, Swiss fondue is made with both Swiss and Gruyère cheeses; this recipe substitutes Cheddar for the Gruyère, and is therefore less expensive.

Rub the garlic around the inside of a heavy-based saucepan, then discard. Add the wine and lemon juice and heat gently, then gradually stir in the Swiss and Cheddar cheeses, a little at a time. Stir constantly until both cheeses are melted and thoroughly combined with the wine. Mix the cornstarch to a paste with the Kirsch, then stir slowly into the cheese mixture. Heat gently until the fondue bubbles and thickens, stirring constantly. Add the cayenne, and black pepper to taste. Pour the fondue into a heated fondue pot and keep hot over a low flame, stirring occasionally. Serve with cubes of French bread. (Guests should spear cubes of bread on fondue forks and dip these into the fondue pot until thoroughly coated in the cheese).

Serves 8–10.

Deviled crab dip

1½ 8 oz packages cream cheese
4–6 tablespoons thick homemade
mayonnaise (see page 20)
2 teaspoons chilli sauce
2 teaspoons Worcestershire sauce
Salt and freshly ground black pepper
1 medium-sized cucumber, peeled, seeded
and finely diced
Pinch of sugar
1 5 oz package frozen crabmeat, thawed
¼ teaspoon cayenne

This is a light creamy dip with a peppery bite. For a stronger flavor of crab, the quantity of crabmeat given here may be doubled.
Beat the cream cheese with a wooden spoon until soft, then gradually beat in the mayonnaise until a soft, creamy consistency is obtained. Stir in the sauces, and salt and pepper to taste.
Sprinkle the diced cucumber with the sugar and stir into the cheese mixture, then fold in the crabmeat. Taste and adjust seasoning, then spoon into a serving bowl, sprinkle with the cayenne and chill in the refrigerator before serving.
Serves about 10.

Blue cheese dip

4 tablespoons unsalted butter, softened
¾ lb Gorgonzola cheese, rind removed and
softened
About 6 tablespoons milk
4 stalks of celery, trimmed, scrubbed and
finely chopped
⅓ cup finely chopped walnuts
Freshly ground black pepper

The Gorgonzola cheese in this dip gives it a strong flavor, and a little will go a long way.
Whip the butter with an electric or rotary beater until light and soft, then gradually beat in the cheese a little at a time until thoroughly combined. Gradually stir in the milk until a creamy consistency is obtained, then fold in three-quarters of the celery and one-third of the walnuts. Add black pepper to taste and transfer to a serving bowl. Combine the remaining celery and walnuts and sprinkle over the top of the dip. Chill in the refrigerator before serving.
Serves about 12.

Serve chilled dips in shallow bowls with a selection of crisp raw vegetables, crackers and potato chips for "dipping". Guests can then help themselves.

Blue cheese dip; Deviled crab dip; Hot cheese and herb loaf

Hot cheese and herb loaf

1 long loaf French bread
4 tablespoons butter
1 8 oz package cream cheese, softened
2 tablespoons finely chopped parsley
2 tablespoons snipped chives
2 tablespoons finely chopped thyme,
marjoram or basil
Salt and freshly ground black pepper

Cooking Time: 15 minutes.
Oven: 400°F.

Cut the loaf in half lengthwise and spread the inside cut surfaces with butter. Beat the cream cheese with the herbs until thoroughly combined, adding salt and pepper to taste.

Spread the cheese mixture on the butter, dividing it equally between each half. Put the loaf back together again, wrap in foil, then place directly on oven shelf. Bake in a fairly hot oven for 10 minutes, open the foil wrapping and continue baking for another 5 minutes or until the loaf is crisp and the cheese is hot.

Remove from the oven, discard foil, cut loaf into thick slices and transfer to a bread basket or board.

Serve immediately.

To freeze: wrap in foil and freeze before baking, double-wrap in a freezer bag.

To thaw: bake in foil from frozen in a fairly hot oven for 10 minutes, then open foil wrapping and bake until crisp and heated through.

Cuts into 12–14 slices.

Celery and walnut salad

2 large heads of celery, trimmed, scrubbed
and roughly chopped
$\frac{1}{4}$ cup chopped walnuts
4 tangerines or mandarin oranges, peeled,
divided into segments and pith removed
6 crisp apples
1 tablespoon lemon juice
$\frac{3}{4}$ cup plain yogurt
1 teaspoon caraway seeds
Salt and freshly ground black pepper

Put the celery, walnuts and tangerines or mandarins in a mixing bowl and stir to combine. Peel and core the apples, then chop roughly. Sprinkle immediately with the lemon juice to prevent discoloration and stir into the celery and walnut mixture. Stir in the yogurt, caraway seeds, and salt and pepper to taste, then mix well. Taste and adjust seasoning, transfer to a serving bowl and chill in the refrigerator until serving time.
Serves 12–15.

Winter salad

1 firm white cabbage (about 2 lb),
shredded
3 large carrots, peeled and grated
$\frac{1}{2}$ cup golden raisins
$\frac{1}{4}$ lb dates, pitted and roughly chopped
$\frac{1}{2}$ lb Edam or Gouda cheese, rind removed
and diced

For the dressing:
6 tablespoons corn or vegetable oil
2 tablespoons lemon juice
2 tablespoons honey
Salt and freshly ground black pepper

Put the cabbage, carrots, raisins, dates and cheese in a mixing bowl and stir well to combine. Put the ingredients for the dressing in a screw-topped jar and shake well. Pour the dressing over the salad and toss until thoroughly coated. Taste and adjust seasoning, transfer to a serving bowl and toss again before serving.
Serves about 12.

Celery and walnut salad; Winter salad; Salata Inglese

Salata inglese

For the dressing:
6 tablespoons olive oil
2 tablespoons red wine vinegar
1 tablespoon Dijon mustard
Salt and freshly ground black pepper

For the salad:
2 heads chicory, washed and broken into
sprigs
2 large green peppers, cored, seeded and
finely sliced
2 heads of fennel, trimmed and finely
sliced
2 hard-boiled eggs, finely chopped
6 oz Stilton cheese, rind removed

Put the dressing ingredients, with salt and pepper to taste, in a large salad bowl and beat well with a fork until thick. Add the salad vegetables and eggs to the bowl, crumble over the cheese, then mix gently together until salad and cheese are lightly coated in the dressing. Taste and adjust seasoning and serve immediately.
Serves 10–12.

Punch; Glühwein

Punch

4 cups rosé wine
½ cup rum
2 tablespoons sugar, or to taste
1 large orange, sliced, pits discarded
1 lemon, sliced, pits discarded
1 cinnamon stick, broken in two
Pinch of grated nutmeg
4 cloves

Cooking Time: 10–15 minutes.

A good drink for Christmas or New Year celebrations. Serve hot in stoneware or heatproof mugs. Pour the wine and rum into a large saucepan, add the sugar and heat gently until the sugar dissolves. Float remaining ingredients on top of punch and heat gently for 10 to 15 minutes. Do not allow to boil. Taste for sweetness, then strain and serve hot with orange and lemon slices in glasses or mugs.
Fills about 8 glasses.

Glühwein

4 cups dry red wine
1¼ cups water
2 tablespoons sugar, or to taste
1 cinnamon stick, broken in two
1 bay leaf
1 lemon stuck with a few cloves

Cooking Time: 10–15 minutes.

A simple Austrian version of mulled wine, Glühwein is the ideal drink to serve with cheese.
Pour the wine and water into a large saucepan, add the sugar and heat gently until the sugar dissolves. Float the remaining ingredients on top of Glühwein and heat gently for 5 to 10 minutes. Do not allow to boil. Taste for sweetness, then strain and serve hot in heatproof glasses or mugs.
Fills 8–10 glasses.

Fresh fruit brûlée

Fresh fruit brûlée

For the sugar syrup:
½ *cup sugar*
⅔ *cup water*
2 tablespoons Cointreau or brandy

For the fruit salad:
4 crisp apples
2 large bananas
½ *lb black grapes, halved and seeded*
4 peaches, peeled, halved, pitted and sliced
4 pears, peeled, cored and sliced
½ *cup blanched almond halves, toasted*

For the topping:
⅔ *cup heavy cream*
¼ *teaspoon vanilla extract*
Scant 2 tablespoons sugar
⅔–1 *cup brown sugar*

Cooking Time: 15 minutes.

The fresh fruit in this dessert will vary considerably from season to season, depending on the availability of fruit. Obviously the best season will be the summer, although good fruit salads can be made in the winter with the help of dried fruits and nuts.

To prepare sugar syrup: put the sugar and water in a saucepan and heat gently, without stirring, until the sugar has dissolved. Increase the heat and boil rapidly for approximately 5 minutes until the mixture is syrupy. Remove pan from the heat and leave sugar syrup to cool. Stir in the Cointreau or brandy.

Peel, core and slice the apples and put in a shallow heatproof serving dish. Peel the bananas and slice thinly, add to the apples with the grapes, peaches and pears. Pour over the sugar syrup, folding it into the fruit with the almonds. Be careful not to break or bruise the fruit. Whip the cream with the vanilla and sugar until thick, then spoon over the fruit in the dish to cover it. Sprinkle the brown sugar evenly over the cream and put under a preheated broiler for approximately 5 minutes until the sugar has caramelized. Remove from the broiler, leave to cool, then refrigerate until serving time.

Serves 8–10.

13

A small buffet party for around 20 people is the ideal
way to entertain relatives and friends informally, and
is particularly suitable for such occasions as
Christenings and Silver or Golden Wedding celebrations.
When planning the menu for your buffet party, try to
choose dishes that allow guests to help themselves. Try
also to provide food that can be eaten easily with the
fingers or a fork, as most of the guests will probably
be standing to eat, and may have to hold a glass of
wine or champagne at the same time.
The recipes in this chapter can all be eaten with a
fork, or a spoon in the case of desserts.

Finger and fork platter

Stuffed cucumbers, eggs and tomatoes, celery boats and
mushroom caps look both attractive and colorful when
arranged on platters for a buffet table, and guests can
easily help themselves. Try to keep individual items as
small as possible so that they can be eaten in one or two
mouthfuls, but provide plates and forks in case some of
the guests prefer not to eat with their fingers.

Stuffed tomatoes
Cut 8 firm but ripe tomatoes in half. Scoop out the flesh
carefully with a teaspoon (this can be used in soups or
casseroles, if liked.) Force $\frac{1}{2}$ lb cottage cheese through a
strainer and mix with $\frac{1}{2}$ cup finely chopped boiled ham
and 1 teaspoon Tabasco sauce (or to taste). Season well
with salt and freshly ground black pepper. Spoon the
filling into the tomato cases, mounding it in the center.
Cut 16 pitted olives in quarters and arrange in a flower
motif on top of the cottage cheese mixture.
Makes 16 halves.

Mushroom caps
You will need 1 pound large cup-shaped mushrooms for
these. Wipe them clean and carefully break the stalks
from the caps. Fry the caps gently in a little butter for 1
minute on each side. Chop the stalks finely and fry until
golden in a little butter with 1 medium-sized onion,
peeled and finely chopped, and 1 cup fine white
breadcrumbs. Transfer to a mixing bowl and stir in $\frac{1}{4}$ lb
finely chopped garlic sausage. Spoon into the mushroom
caps, sprinkle with $\frac{1}{2}$ cup grated Parmesan cheese, and
cayenne to taste, and put under a hot broiler for a few
minutes until golden brown. Transfer to a serving
platter, leave until cold, then sprinkle liberally with
finely chopped parsley.

Celery boats
Trim the stalks of 1 large head of celery, scrub
thoroughly and cut into 2 inch lengths. Beat 1 8 oz
package cream cheese until soft with a wooden spoon,
then stir in 2 tablespoons anchovy paste, $\frac{1}{4}$ cup finely
chopped walnuts, and freshly ground black pepper to
taste. Fill celery pieces with mixture and sprinkle with a
little paprika.

Stuffed eggs
Halve 12 hard-boiled eggs lengthwise, scoop out the
yolks carefully and mash with a fork. Mix with $\frac{3}{4}$ cup
thick homemade mayonnaise (see page 20), 1 tablespoon
curry paste (or to taste), salt and freshly ground black
pepper to taste. Pipe into the reserved egg whites and
decorate each with a slice of stuffed olive.
Makes 24 halves.

Cucumber canoes
Trim 2 cucumbers and score the length of each with the
prongs of a fork. Cut in half lengthwise, scoop out the
flesh from the inside, place in a strainer, sprinkle with
salt and leave to drain for 30 minutes. Pat dry with
absorbent paper towels, then mix with $\frac{1}{2}$ lb shrimp,
peeled, cooked and roughly chopped, 3 tablespoons
thick mayonnaise and 2 tablespoons snipped chives.
Season liberally with salt and freshly ground black
pepper. Cut each cucumber half into approximately 6
"canoes", spoon in the filling and sprinkle each one with
a little cayenne.
Makes 24.

Danish pork and prune open sandwiches

5 large slices of white bread, crusts
removed
Butter for spreading
½ lb canned Danish cured pork
¼ lb cottage cheese with chives
Salt and freshly ground black pepper
10 prunes, halved and pitted
10 large orange slices, peel, pith and pits
removed

The three recipes on these two pages are all variations of Danish open sandwiches and should be made as small as possible for easy eating. Arrange different toppings on the same platter for an eye-catching, mouth-watering spread. Use day old bread or the toppings will not adhere to their bases, and pierce each "sandwich" with a toothpick, if desired. Garnish the platter with sprigs of watercress or parsley.

Spread the bread with plenty of butter and cut each slice neatly into quarters with a sharp knife. Cut the pork lengthwise into 10 slices, then cut each slice in half. Place one slice of pork on each piece of bread, and cut to the same size if necessary. Put 1 heaping teaspoon cottage cheese on each quarter and sprinkle with salt and pepper. Place a prune half on top of the cottage cheese and press down firmly, then cut the orange slices into quarters and arrange two quarters on either side of the prunes to form a "butterfly". Makes 20.

Mackerel salad open sandwiches

6 large slices of rye or wholewheat bread
Butter for spreading
2 4 oz cans mackerel fillets in tomato
sauce, flaked
2 teaspoons lemon juice
2 tablespoons mayonnaise
Freshly ground black pepper

To garnish:
4 hard-boiled eggs, sliced
24 gherkins, drained

Spread the bread with plenty of butter, then cut neatly into quarters with a sharp knife. Mix the flaked mackerel with the lemon juice, mayonnaise and pepper to taste, then spread on the buttered bread, dividing the mixture equally among the quarters. Decorate the top of each quarter with a slice of egg and a gherkin fan.

To make gherkin fans: slice gherkin into four lengthwise, keeping gherkin in one piece at the base. Spread the four slices out in a fan shape, holding the base firmly.
Makes 24.

Danish open sandwiches:
Salami and cheese; Mackerel salad; Danish pork and prune

Salami and cheese open sandwiches

8 oz package (7 slices) pumpernickel bread
¼ lb cream cheese
Salt and freshly ground black pepper
28 thin slices of salami, skin removed
28 pimiento-stuffed green olives, cut in halves

Cut the pumpernickel slices into quarters and spread each one thickly with the cream cheese. Sprinkle with salt and pepper to taste. Fold each slice of salami in half, then cut almost in two. Twist each half in opposite directions then place on the cream cheese, pressing down gently to adhere. Arrange an olive half on each side of the salami. Sprinkle with more salt and pepper. Makes 28.

Avocado mousse

1 tablespoon powdered gelatin
⅔ cup chicken stock
2 ripe avocados
2 tablespoons lemon juice
⅔ cup thick homemade mayonnaise (see page 20)
⅔ cup heavy cream
1 teaspoon Worcestershire sauce
Dash of Tabasco sauce
Salt and freshly ground pepper

To garnish:
1 green pepper, cored, seeded and finely chopped
1 red pepper, cored, seeded and finely chopped
Few tablespoons well-flavored vinaigrette dressing

Light in texture, yet rich to eat, this mousse makes a couple of avocados go a long way. Do not unmold until just before ready to serve or the avocados will discolor. Sprinkle the gelatin over the stock in a small heatproof bowl and leave to stand until spongy. Put the bowl in a pan of hot water and stir over low heat until the gelatin has dissolved. Remove from the heat and leave to cool. Peel and halve the avocados and discard the pits. Mash the flesh with a fork and stir in the lemon juice immediately to prevent discoloration. Stir in the cooled gelatin stock until well mixed, then fold in the mayonnaise.

Whip the cream until thick, then fold into avocado mixture, mixing in the Worcestershire and Tabasco sauces at the same time. Season to taste.

Pour the mixture into a lightly oiled ring mold and chill in the refrigerator for several hours or overnight until set. Unmold onto a serving plate: hold an inverted plate over the top of the mousse, then turn the mold over.

Fill the center of the mousse with the red and green peppers tossed in the vinaigrette dressing.

To freeze: freeze mousse in the ring. Wrap in foil, then overwrap in a freezer bag. Seal, label and freeze.

To thaw: leave in wrappings in the refrigerator overnight, then turn out, fill the center of mousse and serve immediately.
Serves 8–10.

Smoked salmon quiche

For the pastry:
1¾ cups flour
Pinch of salt
¼ lb (1 stick) butter
3–4 tablespoons cold water to mix

For the filling:
1 8 oz package cream cheese, softened
4 egg yolks, beaten
4 whole eggs, beaten
6 oz smoked salmon, slivered
2 tablespoons lemon juice
About 1¼ cups milk or light cream
½ teaspoon cayenne
Freshly ground black pepper

Cooking Time: 35 minutes.
Oven: 375°F.

To make the pastry: sift flour and salt into a bowl, add butter in pieces and rub into flour until mixture resembles fine breadcrumbs. Stir in enough cold water to hold dough together. Form into a ball, wrap in foil and chill in the refrigerator for at least 30 minutes. Roll out the dough on a floured board and use to line an 11 inch quiche pan. Chill for a further 15 minutes.

Meanwhile, make the filling: put the cream cheese in a large mixing bowl and gradually beat in the eggs a little at a time. Stir in the smoked salmon, then add the lemon juice, and enough milk or cream to give the mixture a soft consistency. Stir in the cayenne, and black pepper to taste. Pour the filling into the chilled quiche case, place on a baking sheet and bake in a preheated fairly hot oven for 35 minutes until the filling is set and the pastry golden. Remove from the oven and leave until cold before cutting into wedges to serve.

To freeze: wrap cold quiche in plastic wrap or foil, then overwrap in a freezer bag. Seal, label and freeze.

To thaw: leave in wrappings in the refrigerator overnight. Cuts into 16 wedges.

Avocado mousse; Smoked salmon quiche; Pâté au citron

Pâté au citron

$\frac{3}{4}$ *lb piece boned, skinned ham shank*
6 juniper berries
6 black peppercorns
1 bay leaf
$\frac{1}{2}$ *lb pork, beef or calves liver, ground*
$\frac{3}{4}$ *lb stewing veal, ground*
1 small onion, peeled and finely chopped
1 garlic clove, peeled and crushed
1 cup fresh white breadcrumbs
4 tablespoons lemon juice
1 teaspoon freshly chopped tarragon, or $\frac{1}{2}$
teaspoon dried
1 egg, beaten
Salt and freshly ground black pepper
3 lemons, cut into thin slices, pits removed

To garnish:
Watercress sprigs

Cooking Time: 2 hours.
Oven: 325°F.

Put the ham, juniper berries, peppercorns and bay leaf in a saucepan and cover with water. Bring to the boil, then lower the heat, half cover with a lid and simmer gently for approximately 1 hour or until the ham is tender. Remove from the heat and leave to cool. Remove the ham from the cooking liquid and grind finely into a mixing bowl. Add the remaining ingredients, except the lemon slices, and stir well until thoroughly combined. Lightly oil the base and sides of a loaf tin or earthenware pâté or casserole dish and line with the lemon slices, arranging them as close together as possible. Spoon the pâté mixture into the tin or dish, packing it down well and smoothing with a wooden spoon. Cover with foil and stand in a bain marie (water bath) of hot water. Bake in a warm oven for approximately 2 hours until the pâté is firm and has shrunk away from the sides of the tin or dish. Remove from the bain marie, put heavy weights on top of pâté and leave until completely cold. Turn pâté out onto a serving board or platter and garnish with sprigs of watercress. One or two slices of pâté may be cut before serving, if desired.

Herb and garlic breads

1 long loaf French bread
¼ lb (1 stick) butter, softened
¼ cup finely chopped herbs (parsley, chives, marjoram)

Cooking Time: 15 minutes.
Oven: 400°F.

Cut the bread into 1 inch thick slices without cutting right through the base. Cream the butter and herbs together in a bowl until thoroughly combined, then spread on the cut surfaces of the bread. Wrap the loaf in foil, place directly on oven shelf and bake in a fairly hot oven for 10 minutes, then open the foil wrapping and continue baking for another 5 minutes or until the loaf is crisp. Remove from the oven, unwrap and serve hot.
To freeze: prepare as above, wrap in foil, seal, label and freeze.
To thaw: reheat from frozen in foil wrapping, allowing 5–10 minutes extra cooking time.

Variation
Garlic bread
Prepare as for herb bread, substituting 2 garlic cloves, peeled and crushed, for the herbs.

Beet salad

2 lb cooked beets, skinned and diced
1 cup finely chopped walnuts
2 tablespoons prepared horseradish
2 tablespoons heavy cream or mayonnaise
¼ cup fresh orange juice
Salt and freshly ground black pepper
⅔ cup sour cream
2 tablespoons snipped chives

This colorful salad is simple to make. It has a sharp "bite" which contrasts well with the richness of the Chicken Mayonnaise or Smoked Salmon Quiche.
Put the beets and walnuts in a large mixing bowl and stir in the horseradish, cream and orange juice. Mix thoroughly and season to taste with salt and pepper. Transfer the salad to a serving bowl. Beat the sour cream with a fork until evenly mixed, then trickle over the beets. Sprinkle with chives and chill in the refrigerator until serving time.
Serves 15.

Mayonnaise

1 egg yolk
Pinch of dry English mustard
Salt and freshly ground black pepper
⅔ cup vegetable or olive oil
2 tablespoons lemon juice

When making mayonnaise it is essential to have all the ingredients and utensils at room temperature, or the egg and oil may separate. If separation does occur, start again with a fresh egg yolk, gradually stir in the separated mixture once the mayonnaise is made, then add more oil and lemon juice.
Put the egg yolk, mustard, and salt and pepper to taste in a mixing bowl. Add the oil a drop at a time, beating well after each addition with a fork, electric or rotary beater. When the mayonnaise begins to thicken, add the oil more quickly and eventually pour it into the bowl in a thin steady stream.
When the oil is incorporated, beat in the lemon juice. Taste and adjust seasoning. Cover and store in the refrigerator until required. Let it stand at room temperature before use.

Herb and garlic breads; Beet salad; Mayonnaise

Chicken mayonnaise

1 4 lb roasting chicken
1 garlic clove, peeled and cut in half
4 tablespoons butter, melted
1 teaspoon dried tarragon
Salt and freshly ground black pepper
⅔ cup dry white wine
⅔ cup thick homemade mayonnaise (see page 20)
⅔ cup heavy cream
3 tablespoons sweet mango chutney
2 red dessert apples
1 green dessert apple
1 tablespoon lemon juice
¾ cup blanched almonds, roughly chopped
4 large oranges, peeled and sliced into rings, pith and pits removed

Cooking Time: 1½ hours.
Oven: 375°F.

This salad of chicken pieces in a sauce of mayonnaise and cream looks very attractive when served on a bed of pilaf. See below. Remove the skin from the chicken, rub the flesh with the garlic, then place garlic inside the bird. Brush the bird with butter, sprinkle with tarragon and season liberally. Put the chicken on its side in a roasting pan, pour in the wine and roast in a fairly hot oven for approximately 1½ hours or until the chicken is tender, turning it over onto its other side and its back during the cooking time and basting occasionally. When the chicken is cooked, remove from the oven and leave to cool, then carve into small neat slices or strips. Put the chicken in a large mixing bowl and fold in the mayonnaise, half the cream and the chutney. Core the apples, slice thinly into bite-sized pieces and sprinkle with the lemon juice to prevent discoloration. Mix into the chicken and mayonnaise mixture with half the almonds. Fold gently until all the chicken and apple pieces are coated lightly in the mayonnaise, then taste and adjust seasoning. Arrange the pilaf (see recipe below) on a large serving platter, place the orange slices in a single layer in the center of the rice and spoon the chicken mayonnaise onto the oranges, leaving a border of oranges around the chicken. Trickle the remaining cream in a line down the center of the chicken and scatter the remaining almonds on top.
Serves 10.

Pilaf

4 tablespoons butter
1 large onion, peeled and finely chopped
2 large stalks celery, trimmed, scrubbed and finely chopped
2 cups long-grain rice
About 3 cups hot chicken stock
Salt and freshly ground black pepper
1 large green pepper, cored, seeded and finely chopped
⅔ cup seedless raisins

Cooking Time: 30–35 minutes.
Oven: 375°F.

Cooking rice in larger quantities than given here can be tricky, therefore if more is required it is best to make several casseroles of this size, rather than attempting to cook all the rice in one dish. Melt the butter in a flameproof casserole dish. Add the onion and celery and cook gently until soft and lightly colored. Add the rice to the pan and fry until it begins to turn color, stirring occasionally with a wooden spoon. Pour in 2½ cups of the hot stock all at once, bring to the boil, add salt and pepper to taste, stir once, then cover with buttered wax paper and a lid and transfer to a fairly hot oven. Cook for 30 minutes or until the rice is tender and all the stock has been absorbed. Check the level of the stock after 20 minutes of cooking time, adding more hot stock if the rice is becoming dry. Remove from the oven, leave until cold, then gently fold in the green pepper and raisins. Taste and adjust seasoning. Arrange on a large serving platter and serve with Chicken Mayonnaise (see above).
Serves 10.

Chicken mayonnaise with pilaf; Italian salad

Italian salad

3 lb firm, ripe tomatoes, skinned and
quartered
$\frac{1}{2}$ teaspoon sugar
$\frac{1}{2}$ lb garlic salami, skin removed and
thickly sliced
$\frac{1}{4}$ lb black olives, halved and pitted
$\frac{1}{2}$ lb mozarella cheese, diced
$\frac{1}{4}$ cup olive oil
2 tablespoons lemon juice
1 teaspoon Dijon mustard
Salt and freshly ground black pepper
1 large onion, peeled and thinly sliced
2 tablespoons finely chopped basil or
parsley

Put the quartered tomatoes in a large serving bowl and sprinkle
with sugar. Cut each slice of garlic sausage into small pieces, add to
the bowl with the olives and cheese and stir gently to mix. In a
separate bowl whisk together the oil and lemon juice until thick,
then whisk in the mustard and salt and pepper to taste. Pour this
dressing over the tomato salad, add the onion and basil or parsley
and mix gently until the salad is thoroughly coated in dressing and
herbs. Taste and adjust seasoning, then cover and chill in the
refrigerator until serving time.
Note: If preparing salad ahead of time, do not add dressing, onion
and herbs until just before serving.
Serves 12.

Cheesecake with grapes

½ lb graham crackers (1½ packs)
¼ cup roasted hazelnuts, finely chopped
6 tablespoons butter, melted

For the filling:
¾ lb black or green grapes, halved and seeded
3 8 oz packages cream cheese, softened
2 eggs, beaten
½ cup sugar
2 tablespoons honey
Finely grated rind and juice of 1 lemon

Cooking Time: 1¼ hours.
Oven: 300°F.

The addition of lemon and the garnish of grapes make this rich dessert tangy and refreshing.

Put the crackers between two sheets of wax paper and crush finely with a rolling pin. Put in a mixing bowl with the hazelnuts and melted butter and stir to combine. Using a metal spoon, press into the base and sides of a lightly oiled 7 inch loose-bottomed springform pan. Chill in the refrigerator for at least 1 hour until set. Put a layer of grapes, cut side down, in the bottom of the pan, arranging them as close together as possible. Reserve the remaining grapes for decorating the top of the finished cheesecake. Beat the cream cheese in a bowl until light and fluffy, then beat in the eggs a little at a time. Fold in the sugar, reserving 2 tablespoons, then the honey, lemon rind and juice.

Pour this mixture over the grapes in the pan, then place on a baking sheet and bake in a cool oven for approximately 1¼ hours or until the filling is set. Turn off the oven, leave cheesecake in the oven until completely cold, then transfer to the refrigerator and chill overnight.

Remove cheesecake carefully from pan and transfer to a serving platter. Arrange the reserved grapes in a circular pattern on the top and sprinkle with the remaining sugar.

To freeze: cool cheesecake after cooking, remove springform part of pan, leaving cheesecake standing on base. Freeze uncovered until firm, then carefully ease the cheesecake off the base. Wrap loosely in foil, then overwrap in a large freezer bag. Seal, label and freeze.

To thaw: unwrap, place on a serving dish and leave in the refrigerator overnight.

Decorate with grapes after thawing.

Serves 10–12.

Cheesecake with grapes

Strawberries romanoff

2–3 pints strawberries, hulled and washed
½ cup sugar, or to taste
6 tablespoons vodka
3 tablespoons black cherry jam
1½ tablespoons powdered gelatin
3 tablespoons water
2½ cups heavy cream

This is a light, creamy mixture of strawberries and cream. The addition of gelatin holds the mixture together without setting it as it would in a traditional soufflé. Purée ½ lb strawberries and ¼ cup sugar in an electric blender until smooth. Transfer to a mixing bowl. Mix the vodka and cherry jam until evenly blended, then stir into the strawberry purée.

Slice the remaining strawberries, reserving a few whole ones for decoration, put in a shallow bowl and sprinkle with more sugar (the amount needed will depend on the sweetness of the strawberries). Set aside.

Sprinkle the gelatin over the water in a small heatproof bowl and leave to stand until spongy. Put the bowl in a pan of hot water and stir over low heat until the gelatin has dissolved. Remove from the heat, leave to cool slightly then stir into the strawberry purée. Leave to stand until the purée begins to thicken. Whip the cream until thick, reserving a few spoonfuls for decoration, then fold into the purée until evenly distributed. Gently stir in the sliced strawberries, pour into a glass serving bowl and chill in the refrigerator until serving time. Decorate with the whole strawberries and piped rosettes of whipped cream just before serving.

To freeze: freeze without decoration in the serving bowl if it will withstand the low freezer temperature, or transfer to a rigid container. Cover, label and freeze.

To thaw: leave in wrappings in the refrigerator overnight. Decorate after thawing and serve chilled.

Serves 10–12.

Strawberries romanoff

Anniversary cake

¾ lb (3 sticks) butter or margarine,
softened
2 cups brown sugar
6 eggs, beaten
2⅔ cups flour
Pinch of salt
1 teaspoon baking powder
1 teaspoon ground allspice
1 teaspoon grated nutmeg
1 teaspoon ground cinnamon
¾ lb golden raisin
¾ lb currants
½ lb dark raisins
¼ lb mixed candied peel
6 oz glacé cherries, finely chopped
½ cup blanched almonds, finely chopped
Finely grated rind and juice of 1 lemon
¼ cup brandy, rum or sherry
1½ lb Almond Paste (see page 44)

Cooking Time: 3½ hours.
Oven: 325°F.

Grease a 9 inch square cake pan and line with a double layer of wax paper. Brush with oil.

Beat the butter until soft and light, add the sugar and cream together until light and fluffy. Beat in the eggs a little at a time, adding a little of the measured flour if the mixture shows signs of separating. Sift the flour with the salt, baking powder and spices into a large mixing bowl. Stir in the dried fruit, candied peel, glacé cherries and almonds and mix thoroughly. Fold into the butter and sugar, adding the lemon rind and juice and half the spirits. Mix well together, then spoon into the prepared pan. Spread level.

Bake in a warm oven for 3½ hours or until a skewer inserted in the center of the cake comes out clean. Cover the cake with foil if it becomes too brown during cooking. When cooked, remove from the oven and leave to cool slightly. Prick a few holes in the top of the cake with a skewer and spoon over the remaining spirits. Leave until cold, then turn out of the pan and remove the wax paper. Wrap in aluminium foil and store in an airtight tin for at least a month to improve the flavor, spooning over more spirits from time to time, if wished. Cover with Almond Paste before icing and decorating.

Royal icing

3 egg whites
3½–5¼ cups confectioners' sugar, sifted
1 tablespoon glycerin
Yellow or blue food coloring

The icing is applied to this cake by "flooding" – this method makes it easier to obtain a smooth surface than by the more conventional "flat" icing. Always keep icing covered while not in use or it will become hard and impossible to use.

Put the egg whites in a clean bowl and break up with a fork. Add the sugar a little at a time, beating well with a wooden spoon after each addition. Keep adding the sugar until the icing is smooth and coats the back of the spoon, then stir in the glycerin. Stir gently for a few minutes to reduce air bubbles.

Pour the icing into an airtight container and cover with a lid, or cover the bowl with a damp cloth and place in a plastic bag. Leave to stand for several hours, preferably overnight. Next day, stir the icing gently to reduce air bubbles.

Put ¼ cup icing in a separate bowl, cover with a lid or damp cloth and set aside in a cool place. Color the remaining icing blue for a silver wedding cake, yellow for a golden wedding cake. Stand the cake on a wire rack over a tray and pour all the icing onto the top of the cake. Gently lift and tip the tray to make the icing flow evenly down the sides of the cake and use a metal spatula to help make the icing cover the entire surface of the cake. Gently prick any air bubbles that form on the surface of the icing, working quickly before the icing begins to dry. Immediately scoop up the surplus icing, put in a bowl and cover with a lid or damp cloth. Leave both cake and icing in a cool place overnight.

The next day, run a sharp pointed knife around the base of the cake to make sure that it is free of the wire rack. Put a few blobs of icing on an 11 inch square silver cake board, pick up the cake using the flat of your hands on the sides and place it on the board.

Anniversary cake

Sugar roses

1½ teaspoons powdered gelatin
¼ cup boiling water
About 4 cups confectioners' sugar, sifted
Few drops of food coloring (optional)

Dissolve the gelatin in the boiling water. Stir in enough sugar to make a firm putty-like paste and add food coloring if wished. If storing, keep in plastic.

Pinch out small pieces of paste to form petals, dipping your fingers in a little cornstarch as you work. Wrap these petals around a pyramid of paste, using a little water to make them stick. Make a large rose with eight or ten large petals for the center of the design, then make smaller roses with fewer petals, grading them down to rosebuds with only three or four petals. Cut off the bases of the pyramids at an angle and press onto the cake with small blobs of icing.

To decorate the cake

1. Make a plain wax paper cone and cut it at the end. Thicken the reserved white icing with the remaining confectioners' sugar and put a little in the cone. Mark a 7 inch circle on top of the cake with this icing, then pipe a plain line over the marks to draw in the circle.

2. Draw the outline of the figures "25" or "50", in the center of the circle, using the same paper cone and more of the icing. If wished, you can use packaged numerals.

3. Cut the end of the cone to make a leaf point, put in a little more icing and pipe a garland of leaves on top of the circular line. (Store-bought silver or gold leaves may be fixed between these piped leaves for added effect.)

4. Using the same leaf-pointed cone, pipe a double row of leaves around the base of the cake, one row on the cake, the other on the board. Pipe a few leaves up the sides.

5. Thin down the remaining icing with a little water to a running consistency, put in a small paper cone and use to fill in the numerals in the center of the circle.

If you are planning to cater for a wedding buffet, it is likely to be the most important event for which you ever have to cook, and you will want to be sure that such a special occasion is going to be a success. It is essential to plan your menu several weeks before the day of the buffet. When you have decided on the number of guests to be invited – and they have accepted the invitations – you will have to work out the quantities needed. Each recipe in this chapter has the number of servings at the bottom of the directions, therefore you can easily gauge how many dishes you will need to make for the number of guests that are coming.

Canapés

Ideally, canapés should be small enough to eat in one or two bites. Remove crusts from white, wholewheat or brown bread, toast lightly on both sides and cut slices into halves or quarters or stamp into small rounds with a pastry cutter after toasting. As an alternative to toasting, the bread can be lightly fried in butter – but be sure to drain well on absorbent paper towels before using. If preferred, the canapé base can be made of cheese-flavored pastry – use any recipe for cheese straws, or see recipe for Cheesy Sausage Rolls on page 88. Roll the pastry out thinly and stamp into 2½ or 3 inch rounds and other shapes with a pastry cutter. Another alternative is to use crispbreads or crackers as bases. For an eye-catching spread, combine different shapes, textures and toppings on large serving platters and top with a selection of the following:

Cream cheese toppings
Mix 4 oz softened cream cheese with:
1. ⅓ cup pimiento-stuffed green olives, finely chopped. Season to taste. Spread onto buttered canapés and top with 1 slice of stuffed olive.
2. ¼ cup finely chopped walnuts and ½ teaspoon cayenne. Season to taste. Spread onto buttered canapés and top each with half a walnut.
3. Half a cucumber, peeled, seeded and finely chopped. Season to taste. Spread onto buttered canapés and top each with a generous sprinkling of snipped chives.
4. ½ cup pitted dates, finely chopped. Season to taste. Spread onto buttered canapés.
5. Four slices of crisply fried bacon, finely chopped. Season to taste. Spread onto buttered canapés and top with two strips of green pepper.

Salmon topping
Drain an 8 oz can red salmon and flake with a fork. Fold lightly into 4 tablespoons mayonnaise blended with a few drops of Tabasco sauce. Spread onto buttered canapés, sprinkle with a little cayenne and garnish with watercress sprigs.

Sardine topping
Drain a 4½ oz can sardines in olive oil. Mash well with a fork and combine with 2 teaspoons lemon juice and 2 tablespoons mayonnaise or plain yogurt. Season the mixture with plenty of freshly ground black pepper. Refrigerate for 30 minutes or until needed, then spread onto butter-fried canapés and top each with 2 small onion rings and 1 small parsley sprig.

Tuna topping
Drain a 7 oz can tuna and flake with a fork. Fold lightly into ¼ cup sour cream and season well with salt and freshly ground black pepper. Spread onto buttered canapés and top each with a gherkin fan (see recipe for Mackerel Salad, page 16).

Savory butters
Combine ¼ lb (1 stick) softened butter with any one of the following, blending well with a wooden spoon. Spread or pipe onto canapés and refrigerate until serving time.
Anchovy: Drain a 2 oz can anchovies in olive oil, cover with milk and leave to soak for 30 minutes. Drain well, pound to a paste with a pestle and mortar and blend into butter, with freshly ground black pepper to taste.
Blue cheese: Soften 2 oz Danish Blue/Gorgonzola cheese with a wooden spoon. Blend into butter.
Watercress: Chop 1 bunch watercress very finely and blend into butter. Season with plenty of salt. This butter is an attractive bright green in color.
Chilli: Blend 3 tablespoons chilli relish and the finely grated rind of ½ lemon into the butter, with salt and pepper to taste.

Canapés

Chicken and mushroom vol-au-vents

7 10 oz boxes frozen patty shells

For the filling:
3 tablespoons butter
½ lb mushrooms, cleaned and finely chopped
4 tablespoons flour
2 cups hot milk
⅔ cup heavy cream
½ teaspoon ground mace
Salt and freshly ground black pepper
¾ lb cooked chicken meat, finely diced

To garnish:
Parsley sprigs

Cooking Time: 15 minutes.
Oven: 400°F.

Bake the frozen patty shells following the directions on the package. While they bake, prepare the filling: melt the butter in a pan, add the mushrooms and cook gently for 2 minutes until the juices flow. Stir in the flour and cook for another 1 to 2 minutes, stirring constantly. Remove the pan from the heat and gradually add the hot milk, stirring vigorously with a wooden spoon. Return the pan to the heat and bring slowly to the boil, stirring constantly. Lower the heat and simmer gently until the sauce thickens. Remove from the heat and leave to cool for 1 to 2 minutes, then stir in the heavy cream, mace and salt and pepper to taste. Fold in the chicken meat, return the pan to a very low heat and cook gently until hot.

Taste and adjust for seasoning. Remove the patty shells from the oven, leave to cool slightly, then remove the tops with a sharp knife and reserve. Scoop out any soft pastry with a teaspoon, spoon the filling into each vol-au-vent and replace reserved tops. Garnish each vol-au-vent with a small sprig of parsley, transfer to a warmed serving platter and serve immediately.

To freeze: pour cooled filling into rigid containers. Seal, label and freeze.

To thaw: bake patty shells following the directions on the package. Reheat filling in a saucepan, stirring occasionally. Fill patty shells with hot filling as for fresh vol-au-vents above.

Makes 42.

Salted nuts

6 tablespoons corn oil
6 tablespoons butter
1 lb shelled mixed nuts (almond, peanuts, cashews, walnuts, etc.)
Salt

Cooking Time: 5 minutes.

These make a nutritious nibble with drinks before the buffet food is served.

Heat the oil and butter in a skillet or frying pan until foaming. Add the nuts and fry for 5 minutes, shaking the pan, until browned on all sides. Remove from pan with a slotted spoon and drain well on absorbent paper towels. Sprinkle with salt to taste, allow to cool, then heap into serving dishes or bowls.

Deviled Nuts are a hot spicy version prepared as above with the addition of 1 teaspoon cayenne with the salt.

Other nibbles may be made with dates, prunes and walnuts, stuffed or sandwiched together with well-seasoned softened cream cheese.

Vol-au-vents; Smoked salmon rolls; Stuffed dates; Salted nuts

Smoked salmon rolls

For the horseradish cream:
⅔ *cup heavy cream*
2 tablespoons grated horseradish or
horseradish sauce
1 teaspoon wine vinegar
Salt and freshly ground black pepper

To make the rolls:
1 lb smoked salmon, thinly sliced
15 oz can asparagus spears, drained

To garnish:
Lemon wedges

Smoked salmon wrapped around asparagus in horseradish cream is a luxurious starter for a wedding buffet. To make the horseradish cream: whip the cream until thick, then beat in the horseradish, wine vinegar, and salt and pepper to taste.

Cut the salmon into pieces approximately 3 inch square and cut each asparagus spear in half. Lay the salmon pieces flat on a board, place one piece of asparagus in the center of each piece of salmon, spoon a little of the horseradish cream over the asparagus and roll up the salmon neatly. Arrange on a serving platter and garnish with lemon wedges.

Makes about 34.

Madras shrimp

Madras shrimp

2 tablespoons vegetable oil
2 large onions, peeled and finely chopped
2 tablespoons garam masala or Madras
curry powder, or to taste
1 lb peeled shrimp
Salt and freshly ground black pepper
7 oz can tuna fish, drained and flaked
$1\frac{1}{4}$ cups thick homemade mayonnaise (see
page 20)
$\frac{2}{3}$ cup sour cream
1 tablespoon lemon juice
2 lb long-grain rice, boiled, drained and
rinsed
4–5 tablespoons well seasoned vinaigrette
dressing

To garnish:
1 large cucumber, peeled and thinly sliced
2 tablespoons finely chopped mint

This quantity makes two 9 inch rice rings with a filling of shrimp and tuna in a curried mayonnaise, and it is enough to serve approximately 25 persons as an appetizer. If you wish to make only one rice ring, then halve all the quantities given left. Serve with chilled dry white wine for a refreshing start to a buffet party meal. Heat the oil in a large frying pan, add the onion and fry until soft and golden. Stir in the curry powder and cook for another 2 minutes, stirring occasionally. Stir in the shrimp, with salt and pepper to taste, and cook through. Remove the pan from the heat, transfer curried shrimp to a mixing bowl and fold in the flaked tuna, mayonnaise, sour cream and lemon juice. Taste and adjust seasoning, then chill in the refrigerator until serving time. In a separate bowl, mix the rice with enough vinaigrette dressing to hold it together, then press into two oiled 9 inch ring molds. *Note:* if you only have one ring mold, make one rice ring, refrigerate and turn out, then oil the mold again and make the second rice ring. Chill in the refrigerator for at least 2 hours or overnight if possible. Turn the rice out onto serving platters and carefully spoon the shrimp and tuna mixture into the centers, dividing it equally between the two. Arrange the cucumber slices on top of the rice and sprinkle the mint over the shrimp and tuna filling.
Serves about 25.

Smoked trout mousse

Smoked trout mousse

4 fresh smoked trout (about 1 lb), heads
removed, skinned, boned and flaked
2 teaspoons lemon juice
⅔ cup mayonnaise (see page 20)
⅔ cup heavy cream, lightly whipped
¼ teaspoon cayenne
Freshly ground white pepper
1 tablespoon powdered gelatin
2 tablespoons cold water
2 egg whites

To garnish:
¼ cucumber, sliced
1½ oz lump fish roe
1 tablespoon aspic jelly powder
⅔ cup water

Smooth and creamy, smoked trout mousse is deceptively rich and guests should be advised to help themselves to small portions. Serve with chilled dry white wine.

Put the smoked trout in a mixing bowl and sprinkle with the lemon juice. Add the mayonnaise and stir well to combine, then fold in the whipped cream. Season with the cayenne and white peppers.

Sprinkle the gelatin over the water in a small heatproof bowl and leave to stand until spongy. Put the bowl in a pan of hot water and stir over a low heat until the gelatin has dissolved.

Remove from the heat, leave to cool for 5 minutes, then stir into the trout mixture until evenly distributed. Chill in the refrigerator or leave in a cool place for approximately 1 hour until just beginning to set. Beat the egg whites until stiff, then fold into the mousse. Taste and adjust seasoning, then spoon into a 6 inch soufflé dish, flatten top with a metal spatula and chill in the refrigerator until set.

Decorate the top of mousse with the cucumber slices and lump fish roe. Make up the aspic jelly with the powder and water according to packet directions, leave to cool, then pour over the mousse. Return to the refrigerator and chill until serving time.

To freeze: wrap undecorated mousse in foil, overwrap in a freezer bag. Seal, label and freeze.

To thaw: unwrap and leave in the refrigerator overnight. Decorate after thawing.

Serves 12–14.

Boned, stuffed and rolled chicken

1 roasting chicken (about 5 lb), with the giblets
1 garlic clove, peeled and cut in half
2 tablespoons butter, softened
Salt and freshly ground black pepper

For the stuffing:
Butter for frying
1 large onion, peeled and finely chopped
4 large stalks celery, trimmed, scrubbed and roughly chopped
½ lb mushrooms, cleaned and finely sliced
½ lb chunk bacon, rind removed and chopped
¼ lb pork sausage meat
Liver from chicken, chopped
¼ lb wholewheat bread (4–5 slices), crumbled
½ cup finely chopped fresh parsley
Pinch dried thyme, basil and marjoram
Salt and freshly ground black pepper
1 small egg, beaten
¼ lb stuffed green olives

To garnish:
Watercress sprigs

Cooking Time: About 2 hours.
Oven: 375°F.

Some butchers will bone a chicken for you; if not, then it is quite simple to bone it yourself by following the instructions given below, and it will be so much easier to carve the bird into neat slices at the buffet.

Remove the giblets from the chicken and reserve the liver for the stuffing. Wash the bird thoroughly and dry inside and out with a clean tea towel or absorbent paper towels. Put the bird on a working surface, breast side down. Slit the skin along the center of the underside with a sharp knife, working from neck to tail end. Ease the flesh away from the carcass on one side of the bird, working down to the ball joint. Repeat this process on the other side.

Twist or cut off the scaly end of the leg, then cut through the legs where they join the carcass. Hold the leg bone and scrape the flesh away until the bones come free. Repeat with the other leg and the wings.

Continue to scrape the flesh away from the carcass on both sides, working round to the breastbone. When the breastbone is reached, carefully remove the flesh, being careful not to cut through the skin which is very thin at this point. Lift out the carcass. Lay the chicken as flat as possible on a board, skin side down. Rub the exposed flesh with the garlic clove and season.

To make the stuffing: melt a little butter in a pan, add the onion and celery and cook gently for approximately 5 minutes until soft and lightly colored. Add the mushrooms and continue cooking for another 2 to 3 minutes until the juices flow. Remove the vegetables from the pan with a slotted spoon and set aside in a mixing bowl. Add the bacon, sausage meat and reserved chicken livers to the pan and cook for 5 minutes or until golden brown. Remove from the pan with a slotted spoon and add to the vegetables in the bowl. Stir in the crumbled bread, parsley and herbs, with plenty of salt and pepper, mix well then bind the mixture with the egg.

Spread half the stuffing on the chicken, place the stuffed olives in a layer on top, then cover with the remaining stuffing. Roll up and tuck in the legs and wings. Overlap the skin on the underside and sew the bird neatly together with trussing string. Weigh the bird and calculate the cooking time, allowing 25 minutes to the pound. Place on a rack in a roasting pan. Rub the skin with the garlic clove, then brush with the softened butter and season. Roast in a fairly hot oven for about 1¾ hours, according to weight. Baste and turn occasionally during cooking.

Remove from the oven, leave to cool on the rack, then chill in the refrigerator until firm. Remove the trussing strings, slice the chicken neatly and transfer to a large serving platter. Garnish with sprigs of watercress. Alternatively, the whole chicken may be placed on a serving platter with just a few slices cut.

To freeze: wrap individual slices of chicken in plastic wrap or foil, then pack together in a freezer bag. Seal, label and freeze.

To thaw: leave in wrappings in the refrigerator overnight. Cuts into about 12 slices.

Koulibiac

1½ lb fresh salmon
1¼ cups dry white wine
1 bay leaf, crushed
1 large parsley sprig
4 black peppercorns
Salt
4 tablespoons butter
1 large onion, peeled and finely chopped
¾ lb mushrooms, cleaned and finely sliced
1 cup long-grain rice, boiled and drained
Finely grated rind and juice of 1 lemon
3 tablespoons finely chopped parsley
Freshly ground black pepper
1¾ lb puff pastry
3 hard-boiled eggs, shelled and sliced
1 egg, beaten

To serve:
Large container sour cream

Cooking Time: 1 hour 10 minutes.
Oven: 400°F.

This version of a classic Russian specialty makes a splendid centerpiece for a buffet party table, and is well worth the expense of a fresh salmon.

Put the salmon in a fish kettle or large saucepan, pour in the wine and enough water to cover the fish, then add the bay leaf, parsley sprig, peppercorns and salt to taste. Bring slowly to the boil, then lower the heat, cover with a lid and poach gently for approximately 20 minutes until the fish flakes easily with a fork. Remove the salmon from the kettle or pan, leave until cool enough to handle, discard any skin and bones, then flake the fish. Set aside.

Melt the butter in a pan, add the onion and cook gently until soft and lightly colored. Add the mushrooms and cook for another 2 minutes. Transfer this mixture to a mixing bowl, add the rice, lemon rind and juice, parsley and salt and pepper to taste. Mix gently.

Divide the dough into two portions, one slightly larger than the other. Roll out the smaller portion thinly on a floured board, transfer to a dampened baking sheet and cut into the shape of a fish, approximately 16 inches long and 10 inches at its widest point.

Divide the rice and mushroom mixture into two and spread one half on the dough, leaving a 1 inch margin all round. Divide the salmon in two and lay half on top of the rice. Arrange the sliced hard-boiled eggs in a line down the center of the salmon, then cover with a second layer of salmon and remaining rice mixture.

Roll out the larger piece of dough on a floured board and cut into the same shape as the first piece, but slightly larger. Lay the dough over the filling, seal the edges with a little water and flute them with the fingers or a fork. Brush all over with the beaten egg, make slits in the top to let the steam escape, then bake in a fairly hot oven for approximately 45 minutes until the pastry is golden brown. Remove from the oven, transfer to a serving platter and serve warm or cold. Place the sour cream in a bowl and hand separately.

To freeze: leave until completely cold, then open freeze until solid and wrap in foil or a large freezer bag. Store in the freezer for 1 to 2 days only.

To thaw: unwrap, place on a serving platter and leave at room temperature overnight.

Serves 10–12.

Flageolet bean salad

*2 lb dried flageolet beans, soaked
overnight*
*2 large onions, peeled and very finely
chopped*
*2 large green peppers, cored, seeded and
finely diced*
*2 large red peppers, cored, seeded and
finely diced*
½ lb mushrooms, cleaned and finely sliced

For the dressing:
⅔ cup salad oil
¼ cup tarragon vinegar
¼ teaspoon sugar
¼ teaspoon English mustard powder
¼ cup finely chopped parsley
Salt and freshly ground black pepper

Drain the flageolet beans and rinse under cold running water. Put in a large saucepan with plenty of water (without salt), bring to the boil, then lower the heat, half cover with a lid and simmer gently for 1 hour until tender. Check the water level from time to time during cooking and add more boiling water if it is low.

When the beans are cooked, drain and rinse under cold running water until cold. Turn into a large serving bowl, add the onions, peppers and mushrooms and stir well.

Pour the oil and vinegar into the bowl, add the remaining dressing ingredients with plenty of salt and pepper and toss the salad until the dressing coats the beans and vegetables. Chill in the refrigerator until serving time, toss well just before serving and adjust seasoning.

Serves about 25.

Bean, corn and potato salad

2 9 oz packages frozen cut green beans
1 10 oz package frozen corn
1 10 oz package frozen peppers
Salt
2 lb small new potatoes, scrubbed; or 2
1 lb 3 oz cans new potatoes
*2 bunches scallions, trimmed, washed and
roughly chopped*
*About 1 cup thick homemade mayonnaise
(see page 20)*
1 tablespoon lemon juice
Freshly ground black pepper

To garnish:
2 tablespoons finely chopped mint

Cook the beans and corn in salted water according to package directions, drain, rinse under cold running water and leave to cool. Meanwhile, boil the potatoes for approximately 15 minutes or until just barely tender. Drain, leave to cool for a few minutes, then remove any remaining skin, if desired. Leave to cool completely. (If using canned potatoes, drain, rinse under cold running water and drain again.) Slice thickly or cut into chunks. Put the beans, corn and potatoes in a large mixing bowl with the scallions and fold in the mayonnaise to coat the vegetables completely. Add the lemon juice, and salt and black pepper to taste, then turn the salad into a serving bowl and chill in the refrigerator. Sprinkle with the mint just before serving.

Serves about 15.

Neapolitan salad; Flageolet bean salad; Bean, corn and potato salad

Neapolitan salad

3 large bunches of watercress, trimmed
and washed
2 large heads of fennel, trimmed and
finely sliced
3 lb firm ripe tomatoes, quartered
2 large cucumbers, peeled, seeded and cut
into julienne strips
2 2 oz cans anchovies
4 hard-boiled eggs, quartered
¼ lb black olives, halved, pitted and
quartered

For the dressing:
2 tablespoons Dijon mustard
3 tablespoons boiling water
⅔ cup olive or salad oil
2 tablespoons lemon juice
Salt and freshly ground black pepper

This is an unusual variation of the classic Salad Niçoise. Put the watercress in a large serving bowl, add the fennel, tomatoes and cucumber and mix all the vegetables together with salad forks.

Soak the anchovies in milk for 30 minutes, drain, dry with absorbent paper towels and cut each one in half. Add to the salad bowl with the eggs and olives.

To make the dressing: put the mustard in a heatproof bowl and gradually beat in the boiling water. Add the oil drop by drop, beating constantly until the dressing is thick. Beat in the lemon juice and season to taste with salt and pepper.

Add the dressing to the salad bowl just before serving and toss well. Taste and adjust seasoning.

Serves about 20.

Parmesan ham

Parmesan ham

1 6 lb ham on the bone
½ teaspoon ground allspice
6 cloves
2 bay leaves
2 tablespoons wine vinegar
2–3 tablespoons redcurrant jelly
1–1¼ cups dried breadcrumbs
½–¾ cup grated Parmesan cheese
Freshly ground black pepper
¼ lb (1 stick) butter

To garnish:
Few rings of fresh or canned pineapple

Cooking Time: 2½–3 hours.
Oven: 375°F.

Tie the ham securely with string. Put in a saucepan, cover with cold water and add the allspice, cloves, bay leaves and wine vinegar. Bring to the boil, skim the scum with a slotted spoon, then lower the heat, half cover with a lid and simmer gently for 2 to 2½ hours until the ham is tender when pierced in the center with a skewer.

Remove from the pan, leave until cold, then remove the string and cut off the rind, leaving a thin layer of fat. Brush this surface of the ham with redcurrant jelly. Mix the breadcrumbs and Parmesan cheese together, add black pepper to taste, then sprinkle and press this mixture onto the redcurrant jelly to cover it completely. Place the ham in a roasting pan with the butter and bake in a fairly hot oven for 30 to 40 minutes until the coating is golden brown, basting the ham occasionally with the butter. Remove from the pan and leave until completely cold. Cut a few slices from the ham and arrange with the whole ham on a carving board or platter, garnished with rings of pineapple.
Serves 12–15.

Old fashioned English trifle

Old fashioned English trifle

8 sponge cakes, cut in half lengthwise
½ cup red jam
½ cup sherry
1 package flavored Jell-O
1 package vanilla instant pudding
4 fresh peaches, skinned, halved and stoned
1 tablespoon brown sugar, or to taste
½ teaspoon ground cinnamon
1¼ cups heavy cream

To decorate:
1 oz glacé cherries, halved
Few strips of angelica
¼ cup sliced or slivered almonds

This trifle is best made with fresh peaches when in season, but if unavailable, use canned peach halves.

Spread the insides of the sponge cakes with jam, then sandwich them together again. Put in the bottom of a large, deep trifle dish or glass fruit bowl, pour over the sherry and leave to soak into the sponge.

Make the Jell-O according to package directions, leave until quite cold, then pour over the sponge cakes. Chill in the refrigerator until set. While the Jell-O is setting, prepare the vanilla pudding and allow to cool. Arrange the peach halves, cut side down, on top of the Jell-O. Mix the sugar and cinnamon together and sprinkle over the peaches. Spoon the vanilla pudding over to make an even layer, then chill in the refrigerator until set.

Whip the cream until thick and spread over the vanilla pudding, swirling it with a knife. Decorate the top of trifle, making flowers with cherry "blooms" and angelica "leaves". Arrange almonds decoratively between the flowers. Chill in the refrigerator until serving time.

Serves 12–15.

Tarte française

10 oz flan pastry (page 80)

For the filling:
1 cup sugar
2½ cups water
2 lb fresh apricots, halved and stoned
¾ cup lemon custard
1¼ cups heavy cream
2 tablespoons arrowroot
2 tablespoons rum, lemon juice or water
4 tablespoons sieved apricot jam

Cooking Time: 45 minutes.
Oven: 375°F.

Make the pastry and chill in the refrigerator for at least 1 hour.
For filling: heat sugar and water gently until the sugar has dissolved, then boil rapidly for 5 minutes. Lower the heat, add half the apricots, simmer gently for 5 minutes until tender but still whole. Remove with a slotted spoon and drain. Repeat with remaining apricots. Strain syrup and reserve. Press the chilled dough into a 12 inch fluted flan tin with removable base. Chill for 30 minutes, then prick the base with a fork, cover with foil and fill with dried beans. Place on a baking sheet, in a fairly hot oven for 15 minutes, then remove foil and beans and bake a further 15 minutes until set and golden. Remove and leave to cool.
Spread the lemon custard over the base. Whip cream, then spread over the lemon custard. Arrange the drained apricot halves on top of the cream.
Mix the arrowroot with the rum, lemon juice or water. Return the sugar syrup to the heat, stir in arrowroot mixture and jam, then bring to the boil and simmer until thick. Remove from the heat, leave to cool slightly, then pour over the apricots.
Leave until set before serving.
Cut into 12 portions.

Raspberry charlotte

1 package flavored Jell-O
1 lb fresh or frozen raspberries, thawed
24 sponge fingers
½ cup sugar
4 teaspoons powdered gelatin
2 tablespoons lemon juice
2 tablespoons water
2 cups heavy cream
3 egg whites

Make up the Jell-O with 1¼ cups water. Leave until beginning to set, then spoon half into an 8 inch charlotte mold. Arrange some raspberries on top of the Jell-O and sprinkle with a little sugar. Brush sides of sponge fingers with some Jell-O, then line the mold with the fingers by standing them upright in the Jell-O closely together. Spoon any remaining Jell-O into the mold. Chill until set. Meanwhile, put the remaining raspberries and sugar in a saucepan and heat gently for 5 minutes or until soft. Leave to cool, purée in a blender, then sieve.
Sprinkle the gelatin over lemon juice and water in a bowl and leave to stand until spongy. Put the bowl over a pan of hot water and stir over low heat until dissolved. Leave to cool slightly, then stir into the raspberry purée. Leave until just beginning to thicken. Whip cream until thick, then fold into the purée, reserving some for decoration. Beat egg whites until stiff and fold these in. When Jell-O has set in mold spoon in the raspberry cream. Trim ends of sponge fingers, cover with foil or a plate and chill in refrigerator for several hours.
Note: if the charlotte is difficult to unmold, dip the base of the mold very quickly in a bowl of hot water.
To freeze: freeze in the mold or tin. Cover with foil, overwrap in a freezer bag. Seal, label and freeze.
To thaw: unwrap, unmold onto a serving plate and leave for 4 hours at room temperature.
Three Raspberry charlottes serve 10–12.

2-tier iced wedding cake

This two-tier wedding cake has a delicately pretty design of bunches of grapes and trellis work. The bottom tier will cut into 80 pieces and the top into 50. Follow the instructions for the Anniversary Cake (page 26), baking the rich fruit mixture in a 10 inch round cake pan – this will form the bottom tier of the cake. Make a 6 inch round rich fruit cake using one third of the mixture for the Anniversary Cake – this will form the top tier of the cake. Leave both cakes to mature for one month, spooning over more spirits from time to time. Make the almond paste as in the recipe below and use to coat the 10 inch cake. Make a second batch, using one third of the ingredients, and use to coat the 6 inch cake. Leave both cakes to dry out for one week.

To decorate the cake:

1. Make up the same quantity of royal icing as for the Anniversary Cake (without food coloring), and use to coat the large cake. Prick air bubbles. Quickly scoop up the surplus icing and use to coat the small cake; prick air bubbles. Scoop up any remaining icing, put in a bowl and cover with a lid or damp cloth. Leave both cakes and surplus icing overnight.

2. The next day, lift the large cake onto a 12 inch round silver cake board and the small cake onto an 8 inch round silver cake board. Make up a batch of royal icing using 1 egg white, $1\frac{3}{4}$ cups sifted confectioners' sugar and 1 teaspoon glycerin. Thicken the surplus icing from coating the cakes with more confectioners' sugar until the same consistency as the freshly made batch then mix the two batches together.

3. Fit a piping bag with a No. 4 plain tube, put in some of the icing and pipe a large smooth beading around the base of each cake to neaten it and join it to the boards.

4. Fit a piping bag with a No. 2 plain tube, put in some of the icing and pipe small dots in between the beading, one row of dots on the cakes and one row on the boards.

5. Using the No. 2 plain tube, mark eight tiny dots around the side of the large cake, just below the edge. Space them evenly apart, using a marking ring or wax paper folded into eight. Repeat with the small cake, marking four dots around the side.

6. Take a plain cookie cutter or glass with a diameter of 2 inches and pipe dots of icing around the edge or rim. Press onto the sides of the cake beneath the tiny dots already marked – the dots will adhere to the cake to form circles. Make eight circles on the large cake, four on the small.

7. Using the No. 2 plain tube, pipe parallel diagonal lines across each circle, approximately $\frac{1}{4}$ inch apart. Repeat these lines in the opposite direction, then overpipe both ways to form a trellis. Pipe a small beading around each circle to neaten the edge.

8. Using the No. 2 plain tube, pipe three rough triangles upside-down in between each circle, one large triangle in the center with two smaller ones at each side. Working from the bottom upwards, pipe a small beading all over the triangles to resemble bunches of grapes. Pipe stems to join the bunches of grapes.

9. Make a plain wax paper cone and cut a tiny hole at the end. Put some icing into the cone and pipe random tendrils around the bunches of grapes. Cut the end of the cone to make a leaf point, squeeze out a little icing on a tendril and pull away, releasing the pressure to make a vine leaf. Repeat on all the tendrils.

10. Put four $2\frac{1}{2}$ inch white pillars on the large cake and stand the small cake on top. Decorate the top of the cake with an ornament or small vase of flowers.

Note: for a three-tier cake, make the middle tier with half the rich fruit cake mixture used in the 10 inch cake and bake in an 8 inch round cake pan. Make half the quantity of almond paste and one and a half times the quantity of royal icing.

Almond paste

2 cups ground almonds
$\frac{3}{4}$ cup sugar
$1\frac{1}{3}$ cups confectioners' sugar, sifted
1 egg
3 egg yolks
1–2 tablespoons lemon juice
Few drops of almond or vanilla extract (optional)
About 3 tablespoons strained apricot jam, warmed

Put the almonds and sugars in a bowl and mix well. Beat the egg and egg yolks together with half the lemon juice, and the extract if using. Add to the almond mixture and mix carefully until the paste comes together, adding more lemon juice if necessary. Do not overwork.

Brush the top of the cake with apricot jam. Halve almond paste and roll out one piece on a board sprinkled with confectioners' sugar, to a round slightly larger than the cake. Lift onto the rolling pin and lay over the cake. Trim.

Brush the sides of the cake with the remaining jam. Roll out the remaining paste into a rectangle, long enough to go half round cake and twice as deep; cut into two. Press one piece at a time onto the cake, cutting away any excess along the top. Smooth the joins with a metal spatula, smooth the top of the cake with a rolling pin and roll a straight-sided jar round the sides. Leave to dry for at least one week before icing.

Long summer evenings lend themselves perfectly to garden barbecue parties. Entertaining is simple and fun, the cooking being shared between hostess and guests. Most barbecue dishes are simply marinated and then cooked over charcoal – this gives them the characteristic smoky barbecue flavor. There is therefore very little cooking or preparation to be done before guests arrive. Whether you have sophisticated barbecue equipment or a do-it-yourself arrangement made from a few bricks and a grill, barbecue cooking could not be easier. To be successful, the charcoal must be very hot before the food is placed on the grill, and the coals should burn for about 30 minutes so that the flames die down and the charcoal becomes grey. The grill should be placed on the charcoals from the beginning so that it is very hot when fish, meat or poultry is first placed on it. Always baste the food well while it is cooking.

Hummus

1¾ cups dried chick peas, soaked overnight
2–3 garlic cloves, according to taste, peeled
1 teaspoon salt
About ⅔ cup lemon juice
About ⅔ cup hot water
About ⅔ cup tahini paste
2–3 tablespoons olive oil

To garnish:
2 tablespoons finely chopped mint or parsley

Cooking Time: 1 hour.

Serve this Middle Eastern dip with hot flat Greek or Arab bread known as pita, or, if this is unavailable, substitute crisp French bread. Tahini paste is available at most Middle Eastern shops and health food stores.

Drain the chick peas and rinse thoroughly under cold running water. Put in a large saucepan with plenty of cold water, bring to the boil, then lower the heat, half cover with a lid and simmer for approximately 1 hour or until the chick peas are tender. Drain, rinse under cold running water and set aside.

Crush the garlic cloves with the salt and put in an electric blender with some of the chick peas, lemon juice, hot waster and tahini paste. Blend at high speed until a smooth purée is obtained. Repeat this blending process until all the chick peas have been puréed, adding more tahini paste, lemon juice and hot water to obtain a smooth, creamy consistency.

Transfer to a bowl, beat well with a wooden spoon and adjust the consistency of the hummus with more lemon juice or hot water if it is too thick. Taste and add more salt is necessary.

Pour hummus into a shallow serving bowl, spoon over the olive oil and sprinkle with mint or parsley.

Refrigerate until serving time.

To freeze: leave in the serving bowl without oil and mint or parsley, or transfer to a rigid container. Cover with foil, wrap in a freezer bag, then overwrap. Seal, label and freeze.

To thaw: leave in wrappings in refrigerator overnight, then unwrap and finish with oil and mint or parsley before serving. Serves 10.

Hummus; Lebanese cucumber soup

Lebanese cucumber soup

2 large cucumbers, peeled
Salt
Pinch of sugar
2 garlic cloves, peeled and crushed with ½
teaspoon salt
5 containers plain yogurt
2 teaspoons lemon juice
3 tablespoons finely chopped mint
Freshly ground black pepper

If possible, try to use live Balkan-type yogurt for this uncooked soup. It is normally available from health food shops and its thin consistency makes it the most suitable kind for making soup.

Grate the cucumbers coarsely, place in a strainer, sprinkle with salt and leave to drain for 30 minutes. Transfer to a chilled soup tureen or large serving bowl, add the sugar and stir in the garlic. Gradually pour in the yogurt, stirring constantly, then stir in the lemon juice, two-thirds of the mint, and pepper to taste. Taste and adjust seasoning, then sprinkle over the remaining mint and grind a little pepper over the soup to finish.

Chill in the refrigerator until serving time.

Serves 8–10.

Tandoori chicken

2 2 in pieces fresh ginger, peeled and
chopped
3 garlic cloves, peeled and chopped
3 black peppercorns
2 teaspoons chilli powder
2 teaspoons ground coriander seeds
1 teaspoon ground cumin seeds
½ teaspoon salt
Finely grated rind and juice of 1 lemon
1–2 drops of bright red food coloring
10 chicken breasts or drumsticks, skinned
⅔ cup plain yogurt

To finish:
1–2 heads lettuce, washed and separated
into leaves
3 tomatoes, quartered
1 cucumber, sliced
Salt and freshly ground black pepper

Cooking Time: 20 minutes.

This dish owes its name to the traditional clay oven in which it is
cooked – the tandoor. Cooking on a barbecue makes a very
acceptable substitute as the charcoal helps to give the chicken an
authentic flavor.
Pound the ginger, garlic and peppercorns in a pestle and mortar.
Mix with the chilli powder, ground coriander and cumin, salt,
lemon rind and juice and food coloring. Score the chicken flesh
with the point of a very sharp knife, then rub the pounded mixture
into the skin. Brush each chicken portion with 1 tablespoon
yogurt, then chill in the refrigerator for 24 hours. Let stand at
room temperature for 1 to 2 hours before cooking.
When the barbecue charcoals are hot, place the chicken on the grill
and cook for approximately 20 minutes until the outside of the
chicken is charred and the meat is cooked through, turning the
portions frequently.
Arrange lettuce leaves, tomato quarters and slices of cucumber on
a serving platter and sprinkle liberally with salt and pepper. Place
tandoori chicken on top of salad; serve immediately with yogurt
handed separately.
Serves 10.

Tandoori chicken

Sweet and sour pork kebabs

About 3 lb pork tenderloin, cut into cubes
Salt and freshly ground black pepper

For the marinade:
6 tablespoons vegetable oil
Finely grated rind and juice of 1½
grapefruits
3 tablespoons dark brown sugar
3 tablespoons soy sauce
2 tablespoons black treacle
3 fresh green chillis, finely chopped
1 2 in piece fresh ginger, peeled, chopped
and pounded to a paste in a mortar
1 teaspoon Tabasco sauce

To serve:
Plain yogurt

Cooking Time: 20 minutes.

These hot spicy kebabs should be served with chilled ratatouille and baked potatoes, or hot French bread and a tossed green salad. Put the pork in a large bowl and sprinkle liberally with salt and pepper. Mix all the ingredients for the marinade together, beating briskly to combine thoroughly. Pour over the pork and stir well so that each cube of meat is coated in the marinade. Chill in the refrigerator for 24 hours, stirring the meat and marinade together from time to time. Let stand at room temperature for 1 to 2 hours before cooking.

Thread the cubes of pork onto 8–10 oiled kebab skewers while the barbecue charcoals are heating. When they are hot, place the kebabs on the grill and cook for approximately 20 minutes, turning the skewers regularly and brushing the pork with the remaining marinade.

Serve immediately with yogurt handed separately.

Serves 8–10.

Sweet and sour pork kebabs

Sheftalia

2½ lb boned lean lamb
1 large onion, peeled and chopped
2 garlic cloves, peeled and crushed with 1
teaspoon salt
6 tablespoons finely chopped parsley
1 small egg, beaten
1 teaspoon ground allspice
Freshly ground black pepper
Flour seasoned with salt and pepper for
coating
Vegetable oil for cooking
Few fresh rosemary sprigs

Cooking Time: 10–15 minutes.

These Greek-style kebabs combine ground lamb with onion and garlic. Serve them with yogurt and a tomato and onion salad sprinkled with plenty of finely chopped fresh coriander or parsley. Grind the lamb, onion, garlic and parsley together several times until the mixture is fine and smooth. Stir in the egg and allspice and black pepper to taste and mix until evenly blended. Form the mixture into thin sausage shapes, approximately 2½ inches long, and roll between well-floured hands until the kebabs are firm and lightly coated in flour. Chill in the refrigerator for 24 hours, then thread carefully onto oiled kebab skewers and brush gently with oil. When the barbecue charcoals are hot, put a few rosemary sprigs on the well-oiled barbecue grill. Place the kebabs on top and cook for 10 to 15 minutes, turning the kebabs during cooking, and brushing with more oil from time to time. Remove from the barbecue and serve hot as suggested above.
To freeze: open freeze uncooked sheftalia on trays until solid, then pack in freezer bags or rigid containers and overwrap. Seal, label and return to freezer.
To thaw: cook on the barbecue from frozen, allowing a few extra minutes cooking time until cooked through.
Makes about 40.

Chilled ratatouille

2 large eggplants, sliced
Salt
Olive oil for frying
2 large onions, peeled and finely sliced
2 garlic cloves, peeled and crushed
2 large green or red peppers, cored, seeded
and finely sliced
1½ lb zucchini, sliced
1½ lb tomatoes, skinned, seeded and
chopped
2 tablespoons tomato paste
½ teaspoon sugar
Freshly ground black pepper

This vegetable dish from the Provençe region of France is most often served hot, but it is especially good when served chilled as an accompaniment to hot, spicy barbecued meat and poultry.
Spread the eggplant slices in a single layer on a large plate or board and sprinkle liberally with salt. Leave to stand for 30 minutes, then rinse under cold running water and pat dry with absorbent paper towels. Heat 4 tablespoons of oil in a large saucepan. Add the onion and garlic and fry gently until soft and lightly colored. Add the peppers and fry for a further 5 minutes, then add the eggplant slices, zucchini and tomatoes. Increase the heat and cook briskly for a few minutes, stirring constantly. Stir in the tomato paste, sugar and black pepper to taste, then lower the heat, cover with a lid and cook gently for approximately 40 minutes, or until the vegetables are soft. Remove from the heat, taste and adjust seasoning, and leave to cool. When cold, chill in the refrigerator until serving time.
Serves 10.

Strawberry shortcake

Strawberry shortcake

¼ lb (1 stick) butter
Scant ½ cup sugar
¼ lb roasted hazelnuts, finely ground
1⅓ cups flour
2 cups heavy cream
⅓ cup plus 2 teaspoons confectioners'
sugar, sifted
1½ pints strawberries, hulled and washed

Cooking Time: 15 to 20 minutes.
Oven: 375°F.

Assemble this cake just before serving time. Cream the butter and sugar together until light and fluffy, then beat in the hazelnuts and flour a little at a time. Form the mixture into three equal balls and chill in the refrigerator for at least 30 minutes until firm. With floured fingers, press each ball into an 8 inch circle on parchment paper placed on a baking sheet. Mark one of the circles into eight triangles with a sharp knife. Bake in the center of a fairly hot oven for 15 to 20 minutes or until golden brown (if necessary, bake each circle separately as the pastry will cook too quickly if not baked in the center of the oven). Remove from the oven and cut through the eight triangles of the one circle to separate them. Leave the pastry for 5 to 10 minutes to cool slightly and become firm, then carefully ease off the parchment paper. Leave to cool. Whip the cream until thick with ⅓ cup confectioners' sugar, reserving the rest for dusting. Slice the strawberries, reserving four for decoration, and fold into the whipped cream.
Place one whole round of hazelnut pastry on a serving platter and spread with half the strawberry and cream mixture. Place the second round of pastry on top and spread with the remaining strawberries and cream. Arrange the eight "triangles" on top of the cake, dust with confectioners' sugar and decorate each with a strawberry.
Serves 8.

Pineapple sherbet

Pineapple sherbet

1 ripe fresh pineapple (about 3 lb), cut in half lengthwise
2 egg whites

For the sugar syrup:
½ cup sugar
1¼ cups water

Cooking Time: 10–15 minutes.

Nothing is more refreshing in hot weather than a tangy sherbet or water ice.

Scoop out the pineapple flesh and juice, reserving the pineapple shells, and purée in an electric blender. Transfer to a mixing bowl. To make the sugar syrup: put sugar and water in a heavy-based saucepan and heat gently until the sugar has dissolved. Increase the heat and boil rapidly for 7 to 10 minutes until syrupy, then remove from the heat and leave until cold. Mix the pineapple purée and sugar syrup together, pour into a freezer tray and freeze in the freezer until the mixture becomes mushy.

Turn the mixture into a bowl and beat with an electric or rotary beater. Beat the egg whites until stiff, then fold into the pineapple mixture. Spoon the mixture into the pineapple shells and return to the freezer.

Freeze for at least 2 hours or overnight. Transfer to refrigerator 15 minutes before serving.

To freeze: wrap each pineapple half separately in plastic wrap, then overwrap in a freezer bag. Seal, label and freeze. Unwrap before transferring to refrigerator before serving.

Serves 8.

The most important thing to bear in mind when preparing food for a children's party is that the food must look attractive – children need their appetites stimulated when they are busy playing party games and enjoying themselves.
All the food in this birthday party menu can be prepared well in advance. The ice cream and cakes can be stored in the freezer,
therefore there is no need to be frantically busy in the kitchen at a time when you should be organizing – and joining in – all the fun.

Surprise thatched cottage

1 large white or brown loaf of bread
1 lb cocktail franks, cooked
½ cucumber, sliced
4 oz cream cheese
Potato or cheese sticks
1 stalk celery, trimmed and scrubbed
2 slices of processed cheese

You can fill the bread 'cottage' with any titbits you think your children may like – cocktail franks, potato chips, cubes of cheese and pineapple, miniature sandwiches, nuts, etc. For a small party, use a small loaf.

Cut the top off the loaf and reserve to make the roof. Scoop the bread from the inside of the loaf and fill the hollow with cocktail franks. Place on a board or serving platter. Place the cucumber slices to form a thick layer on top of the loaf. Spread the roof thickly with cream cheese, reserving some for the chimney, windows and doors, then place on top of the cucumber slices.

Press the potato sticks into the cream cheese to form the thatch. Cut the celery stalk in half lengthwise. Sandwich together with cream cheese, press into the top of the house for the chimney, then add a potato stick for the smoke.

Cut the cheese slices into squares to make windows for the front, back and sides of the cottage, and cut two oblong shapes to make front and back doors. Stick these shapes onto the loaf with a little cream cheese and use potato sticks to make frames for the windows, a knocker and letterbox for the front door.

Surprise thatched cottage

Chocolate crispies

¼ *lb milk chocolate, broken into squares*
2 tablespoons milk
2 tablespoons golden or light corn syrup
1¼ *cups cornflakes, lightly crushed*
¾ *cup dried coconut*

Cooking Time: 5 minutes.

Put the chocolate, milk and golden or light corn syrup into a heavy-based saucepan and heat gently until melted, stirring occasionally to mix the ingredients together. Put the cornflakes in a mixing bowl and stir in the chocolate mixture and the coconut. Stir to combine, then divide mixture equally between 12 to 14 paper cupcake cases. Chill in the refrigerator until set, then store in an airtight tin.
Makes 12–14.

Jelly roll

2 8 oz cans pineapple rings
1½ *3 oz packages strawberry or raspberry Jell-O*
Few grapes, stalks removed and washed

You can use a different-flavored Jell-O if preferred, and substitute strawberries, raspberries, mandarin oranges or nuts for the grapes used here. You will need a large empty can to use as a mold–1 lb 3 oz is the most suitable size and it can be kept for future use.
Drain the pineapple rings and measure the juice. Make the Jell-O according to package directions, using the pineapple juice with water.
Pour a little of the liquid Jell-O into the rinsed-out can to just cover the bottom. Chill in the refrigerator until set. Place one pineapple ring carefully on top of the set Jell-O, put a grape in the center, then pour over more Jello-O to cover and chill in the refrigerator until set. Continue making layers of Jell-O, pineapple and grapes until the can is full, chilling each layer until set before proceeding with the next layer. Chill in the refrigerator for 1 hour, then unmold onto a serving platter.
Cuts into 8 slices.

Pear church mice

1 lb 13 oz can pear halves
1½ *3 oz packages lime Jell-O*
21 sultanas, raisins or currants
Angelica

Drain the pears and measure the juice. Make up the Jell-O according to package directions, using the pear juice with the water. Pour into a shallow tin or tray and chill in the refrigerator until set.
Chop the Jell-O roughly with a knife and arrange on a serving board or plate. Arrange the pear halves on the Jell-O, cut side down, then press in the dried fruit to make two eyes and one nose for each mouse. Cut the angelica into very fine strips and stick a few strips on either side of each nose to form whiskers. Chill in the refrigerator until serving time.
Makes 7.

Butterfly cakes

Butterfly cakes

For the cakes:
$\frac{1}{4}$ lb (1 stick) butter or margarine,
softened
$\frac{1}{2}$ cup sugar
2 eggs, beaten
$\frac{2}{3}$ cup self-rising flour
3 tablespoons cocoa powder
1 tablespoon warm water

For the butter icing:
4 tablespoons butter
Scant cup confectioners' sugar, sifted
2 tablespoons water
1 small package chocolate chips

To finish:
Chocolate sprinkles

Cooking Time: 15 minutes.
Oven: 375°F.

Although using only a simple cake mixture and a little butter icing, these pretty cakes never fail to attract children at a birthday party. Cream the butter or margarine and sugar together until light and fluffy, then gradually beat in the eggs a little at a time. Sift the flour and cocoa powder together and gradually fold into the butter and sugar mixture. Beat in the warm water. Divide the mixture between 20 small paper cupcake cases and bake in a fairly hot oven for 15 minutes until risen and golden brown. Remove from the oven and leave to cool. Meanwhile, make the butter icing: beat the butter until soft, then gradually beat in the confectioners' sugar a little at a time, adding 1 tablespoon water when the mixture becomes too stiff to beat. Put the chocolate chips and the water in to a small heavy-based saucepan and heat gently until melted, stirring occasionally. Beat the melted chocolate into the butter icing until evenly distributed.
Cut the tops off the cakes and cut in half. Put a blob of butter cream icing on top of each cake and press in the tops to form wings. Sprinkle each butterfly with chocolate sprinkles.
To freeze: open freeze until solid, then pack in single layers in rigid containers. Seal, label and freeze.
To thaw: remove from containers, transfer to a serving platter and leave at room temperature for 2 to 3 hours.
Makes 20.

Iced cookies

Iced cookies

1¾ cups flour
Pinch of salt
½ cup sugar
¼ lb (1 stick) butter or margarine
1 egg yolk
1–2 tablespoons cold water

For the glacé icing:
¾ cup plus 2 teaspoons confectioners'
sugar, sifted
1–2 tablespoons hot water
Few drops each of bright red, yellow,
green and blue food coloring

Cooking Time: 10 minutes.
Oven: 350°F.

These cookies can be made in any shape you fancy – stars, rings, dogs, cats, etc., and it is now possible to buy sets of fancy cookie cutters at most good kitchen shops. Sift the flour and salt into a mixing bowl and stir in the sugar. Cut the butter or margarine into pieces and work into the flour and sugar with the fingertips. Stir in the egg and enough cold water to draw the mixture together. Form the dough into a ball, wrap in foil and chill in the refrigerator for at least 30 minutes. Roll out the chilled dough on a well-floured board and stamp into approximately 50 shapes with small fancy cookie cutters. Place on greased baking sheets and bake in a moderate oven for approximately 10 minutes until the cookies are set and golden. Remove from the oven and cool on a wire rack. Meanwhile, make the glacé icing: put the confectioners' sugar in a bowl and gradually beat in the hot water, adding enough to let the icing coat the back of a spoon. Divide the icing into three or four and add different food colorings to each. Spread immediately on top of the cookies, then leave to set. If liked, the round cookies can be made into faces with currants for eyes, halved glacé cherries for noses and a curved strip of orange or lemon rind for the mouth. Dogs and cats can also have faces made in this way. Star-shaped cookies can be decorated with edible silver ornaments at each point. Add decorations immediately after icing, then leave to set. Store in an airtight tin.
Makes about 50.

Numeral cakes

For the cake:
½ *lb (2 sticks) butter or margarine,*
softened
1 cup sugar
4 eggs, beaten
1¾ cups self-rising flour
2–3 tablespoons warm water
3 tablespoons jam

For the icing:
10 tablespoons butter
2⅔ cups confectioners' sugar, sifted
2 tablespoons hot water
Food coloring
Cake ornaments, sugared roses, etc.
Candles

Cooking Time: 30 minutes.
Oven: 375°F.

The quantities given left are sufficient to make two cakes to form the number ten. If you are making one of the smaller numbers you will obviously have to trim to waste, but any trimmings can be used for making trifles, or simply eaten by the children!
Grease a 7 inch ring mold and a 7 inch square shallow cake pan. Prepare the cake mixture as in the recipe for Butterfly Cakes (see page 58) and divide the mixture between the two pans. Bake in a fairly hot oven for 30 minutes or until risen and golden brown. Remove from the oven, turn out onto a wire rack and leave to cool. Cut the ring cake in half horizontally, spread one of the cut surfaces with some of the jam, then sandwich the two halves together again. Cut the square cake in half vertically, spread the top of one half with the remaining jam and sandwich the two halves together, one on top of the other.
To make the icing: beat butter until soft, then gradually beat in the confectioners' sugar a little at a time, adding the water gradually as the mixture becomes too stiff to beat. Add a few drops of food coloring according to taste.
Spread the icing smoothly over the two cakes, then press the cake ornaments around the edges. Place candles on top of the cake and make the child's name with more ornaments, if desired.
Instructions for making other numbers:
Two Half of one circular cake, plus one square cake cut and sandwiched together as above, then cut into two pieces, one slightly longer than the other. Trim to shape.
Three Half of one circular cake, plus one square cake cut and sandwiched together as above, then cut into two equal pieces. Trim at the joins and trim to shape.
Four Two square cakes, each one cut and sandwiched together as above. Cut 2 inches off each cake and use the four pieces to make the number.
Five Half of one circular cake, plus one square cake cut and sandwiched together as above, then cut into two pieces, one slightly longer than the other. Trim to shape.
Six One circular cake, plus one square cake cut and sandwiched together as above. Trim to shape at the join with the circle.
Seven Two square cakes, each one cut and sandwiched together as above. Trim at the join.
Eight Two circular cakes. Trim at the join.
Nine One circular cake, plus one square cake cut and sandwiched together as above. Trim to shape at the join with the circle.
To freeze: open freeze without decorations until solid, then wrap loosely in foil or a freezer bag. Seal, label and return to freezer.
To thaw: unwrap, place on a serving platter and leave for 3 to 4 hours at room temperature. Decorate after thawing.

Numeral cake

Whether it is a romantic dinner for two on Valentine's
Day or a more formal party to entertain your husband's
business colleagues, you will want the food to be
something rather special. A dinner party is one of
the few occasions when it is permissible to be
extravagant and use the more unusual and luxurious
ingredients, and it is therefore one of the times
when the cook can really enjoy herself.
All the recipes suggested here are suitable for a celebration.
The first menu in this section serves two; the second serves six.

Goujons de sole with tartare sauce

2–3 small lemon sole fillets,
(about 12 oz), skinned and cut into 1 in
strips
2 tablespoons flour
Salt and freshly ground black pepper
2 eggs, beaten
About 1½ cups dried breadcrumbs
Oil for deep frying

To garnish:
2 lemon wedges
Parsley sprigs

Cooking Time: about 3 minutes.

Sole is traditional for these crisp nuggets of fish deep fried in egg
and breadcrumbs, but for a more economical starter flounder fillets
can be substituted.
Coat the fish in the flour seasoned with salt and pepper, then dip in
the egg, making sure that the fish is thoroughly coated. Coat evenly
with breadcrumbs, then chill in the refrigerator for approximately
30 minutes.
Pour enough oil for deep-fat frying into a deep-fat fryer and heat
gently until the oil is hot enough to turn a stale bread cube golden
in 20 to 30 seconds. Put in the fish, increase the heat and fry for
approximately 3 minutes or until the goujons are crisp. Drain on
absorbent paper towels, transfer to a hot serving platter and
garnish with lemon wedges and parsley sprigs. Serve immediately
with tartare sauce handed separately.

Caneton aux cerises

1 duck (about 4 lb), with the giblets
2 tablespoons butter, softened
Salt and freshly ground black pepper

For the cherry sauce:
2 tablespoons butter
8½ oz can red cherries, drained, pitted and
chopped
2 tablespoons brandy (optional)
2 tablespoons redcurrant jelly
Finely grated rind and juice of 1 orange
⅔ cup duck stock (made with the giblets)
1½ teaspoons arrowroot
1 tablespoon water

To garnish:
1 bunch of watercress
Potato chips

Cooking Time: 1½–2 hours.
Oven: 400°F.

It may seem extravagant to serve a whole duck for two persons, but
duck is a very bony bird and you will find there is very little left
over!
Wash the duck and dry thoroughly with a clean tea-towel or
absorbent paper towels. Brush the duck with the butter and
sprinkle liberally with salt and pepper. Prick all over with a fork
and place on a rack in a roasting pan. Roast in a fairly hot oven for
1½–2 hours, turning over occasionally.
Meanwhile, make the cherry sauce: melt the butter in a small pan,
add the cherries and heat through. Pour in the brandy, if using, and
set alight. Stir in the redcurrant jelly and orange rind and juice,
then pour in the stock. Season to taste with salt and pepper. Blend
the arrowroot and water together, then stir into the pan. Bring
slowly to the boil, stirring constantly, then lower the heat to
simmer gently for a few minutes until the sauce thickens. Taste
and adjust seasoning.
Transfer the roasted duck to a carving dish and garnish with sprigs
of watercress and a few potato chips. Serve the cherry sauce
separately in a sauce boat.

Goujons de sole; Ginger syllabub; Creamed spinach; Caneton aux cerises

Creamed spinach

1½ lb fresh spinach, washed
Salt
2 tablespoons butter
3 tablespoons heavy cream
¼ teaspoon grated nutmeg
Freshly ground black pepper

Cooking Time: 5 to 7 minutes.

Put the spinach in a saucepan with the minimum of salted water. Heat gently until the juices flow from the spinach, then cover the pan and cook gently for approximately 5 minutes until the spinach is tender. Drain well and leave to cool in a colander, then purée in an electric blender or work through a food mill. Return to the rinsed-out pan, add the butter and heat through. Stir in the cream and nutmeg, then season to taste with salt and pepper. Stir gently until the spinach is hot and combined with the cream and seasonings, then transfer to a warmed serving dish and serve immediately.

Ginger syllabub

2 pieces of ginger, finely chopped
2 tablespoons ginger syrup
2 tablespoons medium or dry sherry
2 tablespoons sugar
⅔ cup heavy cream

To finish:
Crystallized ginger, chopped

An old-fashioned English dessert, this Ginger Syllabub is refreshingly light, making a good contrast to a rich main course.
Put the ginger and syrup, the sherry and sugar in a bowl and stir to combine. Set aside.
Whip the cream until thick, then fold in the ginger mixture, making sure that it is evenly distributed throughout the cream. Chill in the refrigerator for several hours, then whip again before serving. Spoon into two individual glasses and decorate with the chopped crystallized ginger.

Fondue bourguignonne with savory sauces

3 lb fillet of beef, cut into 1 in cubes
Salt and freshly ground black pepper
Vegetable oil for cooking
1 garlic clove, peeled and cut in half
(optional)

For the mushroom and tomato sauce:
Vegetable oil for frying
1 small onion, peeled and finely chopped
1 garlic clove, peeled and crushed with ½
teaspoon salt
¼ lb mushrooms, cleaned and chopped
6 tomatoes, skinned, seeded and chopped
Pinch of sugar
Few drops of Tabasco sauce
2 tablespoons tomato chutney
⅔ cup thick mayonnaise
(see page 20)
Freshly ground black pepper

Cooking Time: 8–10 minutes.

This is a simple main course to prepare, and guests love to feel they are giving a helping hand with the cooking. To provide them with fondue forks so that they can spear the meat and cook it to their own liking in the oil over the spirit flame. The cooked meat is then dipped into the savory sauces.

Sprinkle the beef with plenty of salt and pepper and divide into six equal amounts. Arrange on individual plates. Heat the oil slowly in a saucepan on the stove, with the garlic clove (if using). When very hot, pour into a fondue pot and keep hot over a spirit flame on the table. Hand sauces separately; stir before serving.

To make the mushroom and tomato sauce: heat a little oil in a pan, add the onion and garlic and cook gently for approximately 5 minutes until soft and lightly colored. Add the mushrooms and tomatoes, increase the heat and cook another few minutes until the mixture thickens and reduces. Remove from the heat, leave to cool, then stir in the remaining ingredients with pepper to taste. Taste and adjust seasoning. Chill in the refrigerator until serving time.

To make the mustard sauce: mix 1 tablespoon Dijon mustard together with ⅔ cup mayonnaise and a little heavy cream. Season, stir and chill.

To make the anchovy sauce: drain 1 small can anchovies and pound to a paste, mix with ⅔ cup mayonnaise; add capers and seasoning to taste. Chill in the refrigerator until serving time.

Smoked haddock crêpes

1¼ cups crêpe batter (see page 86)

For the filling:
4 tablespoons butter
⅓ cup flour
2 cups hot milk
¼ teaspoon ground mace
¾ cup grated Parmesan cheese
Freshly ground white pepper
¾ lb smoked haddock, poached in milk,
drained, boned and flaked

Cooking Time: 25 minutes.

This is an unusual and quite substantial appetizer. Two crêpes per person is an ample serving.

Make 12 crêpes as in the method on page 86 and keep them warm. To make the filling: melt the butter in a pan, stir in the flour and cook gently for 1 to 2 minutes, stirring constantly. Remove from the heat and gradually add the hot milk, stirring vigorously. When all the milk is incorporated, return the pan to the heat and bring to the boil, stirring constantly. Lower the heat, add the mace, two-thirds of the Parmesan cheese, and pepper to taste. Simmer gently until the sauce is thick, stirring constantly. Taste and adjust seasoning.

Remove the pan from the heat and pour approximately half the sauce into a mixing bowl. Fold in the flaked fish. Lay the crêpes flat on a board or working surface and put a spoonful of filling on each one. Roll up the crêpes and place in a single layer in a shallow heatproof serving dish. Pour over the remaining sauce, sprinkle with the remaining Parmesan cheese and put under a preheated hot grill for a few minutes until the top is golden brown. Serve hot straight from the dish.

French potato casserole

French potato casserole

About 3 lb potatoes, peeled
Salt
4 tablespoons butter, softened
Freshly ground black pepper
6 tablespoons milk
6 tablespoons light cream
½ cup grated Swiss cheese

Cooking Time: 1 hour.
Oven: 375°F.

This casserole makes a substantial vegetable dish to serve with Fondue Bourguignonne, and no other vegetable should be needed apart from a green salad.

Blanch the potatoes in boiling salted water for 5 minutes, then drain and leave until cool enough to handle. Slice the potatoes thickly.

Brush the inside of a large casserole dish with some of the butter. Arrange a layer of potato slices in the bottom, sprinkle with salt and pepper and dot with some more of the butter. Pour in 1 tablespoon each of milk and cream. Continue with these layers until all the ingredients are used up, pouring in any remaining milk and cream at the end. Sprinkle the top of casserole with the grated cheese and more salt and pepper.

Bake, uncovered, in a fairly hot oven for about 1 hour until the top is golden brown and the potatoes are tender when pierced. Serve hot straight from the casserole.

Crème brûlée with sugared raspberries

Crème brûlée with sugared raspberries

$\frac{1}{2}$ *cup sugar*
2 teaspoons vanilla extract
6 egg yolks
3$\frac{3}{4}$ cups heavy cream
$\frac{1}{3}$ cup brown sugar
$\frac{3}{4}$ lb fresh or frozen raspberries, thawed

Cooking Time: 1$\frac{1}{4}$ hours.
Oven: 300°F.

Any soft summer fruit can be substituted for the raspberries that top this dessert.

Put two-thirds of the sugar, the vanilla extract and egg yolks in a bowl and beat to combine without allowing to become frothy. Set aside.

Put the cream in the top of a double boiler or in a heatproof bowl standing on top of a pan of gently simmering water. Heat until just below boiling point, then immediately pour into the egg yolk mixture, stirring to combine. Strain into a baking dish and put in a bain marie or roasting pan half filled with hot water.

Bake in a cool oven for 1$\frac{1}{4}$ hours or until just set. Remove dish from bain marie, leave until cold, then chill in the refrigerator, overnight if possible. When chilled, sprinkle with the brown sugar and put under a preheated broiler until the sugar caramelizes.

Remove from broiler and leave to cool again. Meanwhile, toss the raspberries in the remaining sugar. Cover the top of the crème brûlée with the sugared raspberries and serve chilled straight from the baking dish.

Easter is second only to Christmas in being one of the most celebrated of Christian festivals, yet many of our Easter customs are pagan in origin. Hot Cross Buns are believed to have been eaten before Christian times when the cross was made to depict the sun and the fire. Nowadays, Hot Cross Buns and Easter Cookies are traditionally eaten on Good Friday, the cross on the buns being of religious significance; and roast spring lamb is served for lunch on Easter Sunday to represent the innocence of Christ.

Hot cross squares

1 oz fresh yeast, or 4 teaspoons dry active yeast and 1 teaspoon sugar
1¼ cups warm milk and water mixed
1 lb (3½ cups) flour
1 teaspoon salt
½ teaspoon ground allspice
½ teaspoon ground cinnamon
½ teaspoon grated nutmeg
¼ cup sugar
4 tablespoons butter
1 egg, beaten
½ cup currants
½ cup chopped mixed peel

To finish:
Shortcrust pastry dough (made with ¾ cup flour, 4 tablespoons butter, 1 tablespoon water)
¼ cup sugar
2 tablespoons water

Cooking Time: 20 minutes.
Oven: 375°F.

This is a simple variation of the traditional hot cross buns. If you prefer, you can still form the dough into bun shapes and bake on greased baking sheets.

Cream the fresh yeast with a little of the milk and water. (If using dried yeast, stir the sugar into the milk and water and sprinkle the dried yeast over. Leave in a warm place for 10 minutes or until frothy.)

Meanwhile sift the flour, salt and spices into a warm mixing bowl. Stir in the sugar. Rub in the butter with the fingertips. Make a well in the center of the flour, pour in the frothy yeast mixture and liquid, the egg, currants and mixed peel. Mix together with the hands until a soft dough is formed. Turn out onto a lightly floured board and knead for 10 minutes until smooth. Roll out the dough to a rectangle to fit a roasting pan about 12 × 9 inches, brush the inside of the pan with butter and put in the dough. Mark into twelve squares with a sharp knife. Leave in a warm place for approximately 1 hour until almost doubled in bulk.

Roll out the shortcrust pastry dough on a floured board and cut into three 12 inch strips and four 9 inch strips. Place the strips on top of the risen dough, forming a criss-cross pattern to make crosses on the twelve squares. Use a little water to stick the strips on. Bake in the center of a fairly hot oven for 20 minutes or until browned on top. Remove from the oven, leave to cool for a few minutes, then cut into twelve squares. Transfer squares to a wire rack.

Put the sugar and water into a heavy-based pan and heat gently until the sugar has dissolved. Increase the heat and boil rapidly for a few minutes until a syrup is formed. Remove from the heat and brush over the squares until all the syrup is used. Leave until cool before splitting in two and spreading with butter.

To freeze: open freeze until solid, then pack in a single layer in rigid containers or freezer bags. Seal, label and return to freezer.

To thaw: leave in wrappings for about 45 minutes at room temperature, then unwrap, place on a baking sheet and refresh in a fairly hot oven for 5 to 10 minutes until warmed through.

Makes 12.

Carrot and tomato soup

2 tablespoons butter
1 large onion, peeled and finely chopped
1 lb carrots, scraped and chopped
16 oz can tomatoes
1 teaspoon sugar
2½ cups chicken stock
Finely grated rind and juice of 1 orange
Salt and freshly ground black pepper

To garnish:
3 tablespoons finely chopped parsley

Cooking Time: 25 to 30 minutes.

Sweet, young carrots give this soup its refreshing flavor and light texture.

Melt the butter in a heavy saucepan, add the onion and cook gently for approximately 5 minutes until soft and lightly colored. Stir in the carrots, cover the vegetables with wax paper, then cover the pan and cook over a very low heat for another 5 minutes.
Remove the lid and wax paper, stir in the tomatoes, sugar, stock, orange rind and juice and season to taste with salt and pepper. Bring to the boil, stirring, then lower the heat, half cover with the lid and simmer for 10 to 15 minutes until the carrots are tender. Remove from the heat and leave to cool a little. Purée in an electric blender or work through a food mill until smooth. Return the soup to the rinsed-out pan and heat through. If the soup is too thick, stir in a little chicken stock, milk or water. Taste and adjust seasoning. Pour into warmed soup bowls and sprinkle each with a little parsley. Serve immediately.
To freeze: pour cooled soup into a rigid container, leaving head space. Seal, label and freeze.
To thaw: reheat soup from frozen in a saucepan over gentle heat, stirring constantly. Garnish with parsley just before serving.
Serves 4–6.

Tarte au citron; Carrot and tomato soup; Spiced leg of lamb

Spiced leg of lamb

1 4 lb leg of lamb
1 garlic clove, peeled and cut into slivers
1 tablespoon ground coriander
1 tablespoon ground cumin
1 tablespoon flour
6 black peppercorns, crushed
1 teaspoon salt
2 tablespoons tomato paste
2 teaspoons lemon juice
4 tablespoons lard or drippings (melted beef fat)
2 cups hot beef stock

Cooking Time: $1\frac{3}{4}$ hours.
Oven: 450°F, then reduce to 350°F.

Serve this leg of lamb with a medley of fresh spring vegetables – imported new potatoes, peas and carrots.
Score the skin of the lamb and insert the garlic slivers. Mix together the spices, flour, peppercorns, salt, tomato paste and lemon juice in a bowl and brush all over the lamb. Chill in the refrigerator overnight. Put the lamb in a roasting pan with the lard or drippings. Roast on the top shelf of a very hot oven for 15 to 20 minutes until the meat is browned, basting occasionally. Pour the hot stock into the pan, lower the heat to moderate and roast for approximately $1\frac{1}{2}$ hours or until the juices run pink when the meat is pierced with a skewer. Spoon the stock over the lamb from time to time during cooking.
Remove the meat from the pan and let rest before carving. Transfer the pan to the top of the stove and boil the stock to reduce to a thick gravy. Taste and adjust seasoning before serving.
Serves 4–6.

Tarte au citron

Sweet shortcrust pastry (see Mincemeat flan, page 80)

For the filling:
4 tablespoons butter
Finely grated rind and juice of 2 lemons
2 eggs, beaten
1 cup sugar
6 tablespoons ground almonds

For the topping:
2 lemons, thinly sliced, pits removed

For the glaze:
Water
1 cup sugar

Cooking Time: 20–25 minutes.
Oven: 375°F.

Roll out the shortcrust pastry and line an 8 inch flan dish or flan ring placed on a baking sheet. Flute the edges and prick the base, then chill the dough in the refrigerator for another 30 minutes. Line the dough with foil and dried beans and bake blind in a fairly hot oven for 10 minutes. Remove foil and beans, return to the oven and bake for another 10 to 15 minutes until the pastry is golden and set. Remove and leave to cool.
Put the ingredients for the filling (except the ground almonds) in the top of a double boiler or in a heatproof bowl standing over a pan of gently simmering water. Cook the mixture for 30 to 40 minutes until thick, stirring constantly with a wooden spoon. Remove from the heat and stir in the ground almonds until evenly mixed. Pour into the flan case and leave to set in a cool place overnight. Meanwhile, prepare the lemon slices for the top of the tart. Put the slices in a heatproof bowl, pour over boiling water to cover and leave overnight. The next day, drain the slices, put in a pan and cover with fresh water. Bring to the boil and simmer gently for 20 to 30 minutes until they are soft. Remove lemon slices with a slotted spoon, reserving the cooking liquid. Dry on absorbent paper towels, then arrange on top of the set filling.
To prepare the glaze: make the reserved cooking liquid from the lemon slices up to $1\frac{1}{4}$ cups with water. Put in a heavy-based pan with the sugar and heat gently until the sugar has dissolved. Increase the heat and boil rapidly for 7 to 10 minutes until syrupy. Remove from the heat, leave to cool slightly, then spoon over the lemon slices to cover. Leave to set, then remove flan ring, if used. Place flan on a serving platter before serving.
Serves 4–6.

Colored eggs

Colored eggs

These are traditional at Easter – particularly in Eastern Europe – and are very simple to make. If you wish to paint decorations or elaborate designs on eggs, then you must hard-boil them for 12 minutes before working on them. Eggs can be left white or colored by steeping in fabric dyes after hard-boiling. Use fine-nibbed felt tip pens for decorating eggs, etching in the design with a faint pencil beforehand. Allow each side of the egg to dry before working round the egg. Hard-boiled eggs will keep indefinitely if the shells are kept intact, and they make a most attractive Easter decoration.

To color eggs with food coloring: put 2 teaspoons food coloring – red, cochineal, blue, yellow etc. – into a saucepan of boiling water and stir well. Put in the quantity of white-shelled eggs you wish to color and boil for 10 minutes or until the egg shells become colored. The eggs will take on delicate, pale colors which can be improved by rubbing gently with a little oil after the eggs have cooled.

To color eggs yellow or rust with onion skins: put the skins of several onions in a pan with plenty of cold water (add 2 teaspoons malt vinegar for a rust color). Bring to the boil, then simmer gently until the water becomes colored. The longer the skins are simmered, the deeper the color. Strain into a bowl. Put hard-boiled white eggs into the strained liquid and leave to steep until the desired color is obtained. Remove from the liquid with a slotted spoon, pat dry with absorbent kitchen towels, then brush lightly with oil and buff with more paper or a duster. Leave plain or decorate as above and keep indefinitely.

Paskha

Paskha

½ cup maraschino cherries, drained and
chopped
½ cup chopped mixed peel
½ cup blanched almonds, finely chopped
½ cup seedless raisins
Finely grated rind of 1 lemon
1 tablespoon dry sherry
¾ lb cottage cheese
¼ lb cream cheese
½ cup sugar
½ cup heavy cream
2 teaspoons powdered gelatin
3 tablespoons lemon juice

To garnish:
A little oil
About 12 glacé cherries, halved

Paskha is a Russian Easter specialty, a kind of uncooked
cheesecake mixed with fruit and nuts. This is a simplified version
and is delicious served for a dessert, or at teatime.
Put the maraschino cherries, mixed peel, almonds, raisins and
lemon rind in a small bowl, stir in the sherry and mix well until the
sherry is absorbed. Set aside.
Mix the cottage and cream cheeses together, then beat in the sugar.
Beat the cream until thick and fold into the cheese with the fruit
and nut mixture.
Sprinkle the gelatin over the lemon juice in a small heatproof bowl,
leave until spongy, then place the bowl in a pan of hot water and
stir over low heat until the gelatin has dissolved. Remove from the
heat, leave to cool slightly, then fold into the cheese mixture. Line
a 5 inch clay flower pot with a large piece of muslin or a clean tea-
towel, spoon in the cheese and fold the cloth over the top. Cover
with a saucer, place heavy weights on top, stand in a bowl and chill
in the refrigerator overnight.
The next day, remove the weights and saucer and unfold the cloth.
Invert a serving platter over the pot and turn out the paskha. Brush
lightly with oil, then press halved glacé cherries around the top and
bottom edges. Chill in the refrigerator until serving time.
Serves 6–8.

French Easter cake

For the Genoese sponge:
$\frac{2}{3}$ cup flour
3 tablespoons cornstarch
4 eggs, beaten
$\frac{1}{2}$ cup sugar
$\frac{1}{4}$ lb (1 stick) unsalted butter, melted and cooled

For the butter icing:
12 tablespoons butter
1 lb confectioners' sugar, sifted
2 tablespoons hot water
4 oz semi-sweet chocolate, broken into pieces
2 tablespoons strong coffee

To finish:
Few miniature Easter eggs

Cooking Time: 20–25 minutes.
Oven: 375°F.

To make the sponge: grease three 7 inch round shallow cake pans and line the bases.

Sift the flour and cornstarch together and set aside. Put the eggs and sugar in a heatproof bowl and stand over a pan of simmering water. Beat with a balloon whisk, electric or rotary beater until the mixture becomes thick. Remove from the heat and continue beating until the mixture is cool. Slowly stir the melted butter into the mixture from the side of the bowl, then sift half the flour and cornstarch over the bowl and fold in gently. Repeat with the remaining flour and cornstarch.

Pour the mixture into the prepared pans and bake in the center of a fairly hot oven for 20 to 25 minutes, until well risen and firm to the touch.

Meanwhile, make the butter cream: beat the butter in a bowl until light, then gradually beat in the confectioners' sugar a little at a time, adding hot water as the mixture becomes too stiff to beat. Put one quarter of the butter cream in a separate bowl. Set aside. Put the chocolate pieces and coffee in a heatproof bowl and stand over a pan of gently simmering water. Heat gently until the chocolate has melted, stirring occasionally, then remove from the heat and stir into the separate quarter of butter cream. Spread some of this chocolate butter cream on top of two of the cakes and sandwich the three cakes together. Put the cake on a stand and spread the top and sides with most of the unflavored butter cream.

Stir the leftover unflavored butter cream into the remaining chocolate butter cream and put into a pastry bag fitted with a small star tube. Pipe small stars around the top edge of the cake and join the stars together by piping a line between each one. Pipe vertical lines around the sides of the cake beneath the stars, working from the bottom upwards. Repeat the top edge decoration around the bottom of the cake and decorate with Easter eggs.

Cuts into 8–10 slices.

Easter cookies

6 tablespoons butter or margarine
Scant $\frac{1}{2}$ cup sugar
1 egg, beaten
$1\frac{1}{3}$ cups self-rising flour
Pinch of salt
$\frac{1}{2}$ teaspoon ground allspice
$\frac{1}{2}$ cup currants
1–2 tablespoons milk

To finish:
1 egg white, lightly beaten
Superfine sugar for sprinkling

Cooking Time: 20 minutes.
Oven: 350°F.

Cream together the butter or margarine and sugar in a mixing bowl until light and fluffy, then beat in the egg. Sift the flour, salt and allspice and fold into the creamed mixture with the currants. Beat well to mix, adding enough milk to make a soft pliable dough. Knead lightly until the dough is smooth, then roll out on a floured board to $\frac{1}{4}$ inch thick. Stamp into rounds. Put cookies on greased baking sheets, allowing room for expansion. Bake in the center of a moderate oven for 10 minutes. Remove from the oven, brush with the egg white and sprinkle with superfine sugar. Return to the oven and continue cooking for another 10 minutes or until the cookies are golden and crisp. When cooked, leave cookies to cool for a few minutes. Transfer to a wire rack to cool completely. Store in an airtight tin.

Makes 16–18.

Everyone looks forward to the traditional fare of Christmastide
and the Christmas dinner should be a meal to remember.
In Great Britain ever since Elizabethan days, roast goose has been
the traditional bird for the Christmas table. The recipe for
Roast Goose with two stuffings in this chapter will be ample for six,
but if you have a larger gathering it would perhaps be wiser
to serve turkey – a far meatier bird than goose and one that will
provide you with many more meals for the days after Christmas.
If you are entertaining at Christmas you will obviously have to
plan all the meals down to the last detail. Both the Plum Pudding
and the Christmas Cake can be made long before the festive
season – plum pudding will keep for as long as 12 months, or more if
stored in a cool, dry place; so too will the cake without its almond
paste and royal icing.

Roast goose with stuffings

*1 9 lb goose, trussed and cleaned, with
giblets*
2 tablespoons honey
Salt and freshly ground black pepper

For the sausage meat and apple stuffing:
2 tablespoons butter
*2 medium-sized onions, peeled and finely
chopped*
Liver from goose, finely chopped
½ lb pork sausage meat
2 large cooking apples
2½ cups wholewheat breadcrumbs

For the sage and onion stuffing:
4 tablespoons butter
1 lb onions, peeled and finely chopped
5 cups fresh white breadcrumbs
1 egg, beaten
3 tablespoons dried sage
3–4 tablespoons light cream

Cooking Time: 3–3½ hours.
Oven: 400°F, then reduce to 350°F.

The traditional stuffing for Christmas roast goose is sage and
onion, but sausage meat and apple makes an unusual alternative.
Choose one or the other, or stuff the goose with sausage meat and
apple, then form the sage and onion into small balls, coat in flour
and shallow fry until crisp. Arrange around the goose when
serving. To make the sausage meat and apple stuffing: melt the
butter in a pan, add the onions and cook gently until golden. Add
the liver and sausage meat and cook until browned, breaking up
and stirring constantly. Peel, core and chop the apples and add to
the pan. Continue cooking for 5 minutes, stirring constantly, then
transfer to a bowl and stir in the breadcrumbs. Season and mix
well.

To make the sage and onion stuffing: melt the butter in a pan, add
the onions and cook gently until golden. Transfer to a bowl and stir
in the breadcrumbs, egg and sage. Mix well, adding enough cream
or milk to hold the stuffing together. Season to taste with salt and
pepper. Spoon the chosen stuffing into the cavity of the goose, then
sew up both openings with trussing string. Secure with skewers if
necessary. Place the goose on a rack in a roasting pan, brush with
the honey and sprinkle liberally with salt and pepper. Roast in a
fairly hot oven for 30 minutes to brown the skin, then cover the
bird with foil, reduce the heat to moderate and roast for another 2½
to 3 hours or until the juices run clear when the goose is pierced
with a skewer. Baste and turn the bird frequently during cooking,
and pour off excess fat. Remove the bird from the oven and discard
strings and skewers, if used. Transfer to a warmed serving platter
and serve with roast potatoes, seasonal vegetables and a well-
flavored giblet gravy made with the pan juices.
Serves 6.

Bread sauce; Cranberry sauce

Cranberry sauce

½ lb fresh or frozen cranberries
½–¾ cup sugar
Finely grated rind and juice of 1 orange

Cooking Time: 30 minutes.

The sharp flavor of cranberries with a hint of sweet orange makes a welcome contrast to the richness of other Christmas fare.
Put the cranberries in a pan, stir in ½ cup of the sugar and the orange rind and juice. Pour in enough water to just cover the fruit and bring to the boil. Lower the heat and simmer the sauce gently for about 30 minutes until the cranberries are tender and split open. Remove sauce from the heat, leave to cool slightly, then rub through a sieve. Taste and add more sugar if necessary. Pour into a serving bowl and chill in the refrigerator until serving time.
To freeze: cover bowl with plastic wrap and pack in a freezer bag. Or transfer sauce to a rigid container. Seal, label and freeze.
To thaw: leave in wrappings at room temperature for 3–4 hours.
Serves 6.

Bread sauce

1 onion, peeled and stuck with 6 cloves
2 cups milk
¼ teaspoon ground mace
6 black peppercorns, crushed
1 bay leaf, crushed
½ teaspoon salt
2 cups fresh white breadcrumbs
2 tablespoons butter

Cooking Time: 5–7 minutes.

A flavorsome bread sauce is an essential part of the traditional festive table. Serve it with roast chicken, turkey or pheasant.
Put the onion in a pan, pour in the milk, then add the mace, peppercorns, bay leaf and salt. Bring slowly to the boil, then turn off the heat, cover the pan with a lid and leave to infuse for 15 to 20 minutes. Strain the milk, then return to the rinsed-out pan, add the breadcrumbs and butter and simmer gently until hot and thickened, stirring occasionally. Taste and adjust seasoning before serving.
Serves 6.

Rum butter; Brandy butter

Brandy and rum butters

$\frac{1}{4}$ *lb (1 stick) unsalted butter, softened*
$\frac{3}{4}$ cup plus 1 tablespoon confectioners' sugar, sifted
Finely grated rind and juice of 1 lemon
3–4 tablespoons brandy

Rich plum pudding topped with lashings of brandy or rum butter is traditional at Christmas time, and home-made butters are far superior to any of the commercial varieties available.

Put the butter in a mixing bowl and beat until light and fluffy. Gradually add the confectioners' sugar a little at a time, beating vigorously until all is incorporated. Beat in the lemon rind and juice, and brandy to taste. Spoon into a serving bowl and chill in the refrigerator until needed.

To freeze: cover bowl with plastic wrap or foil and pack in a freezer bag. Or transfer butter to a rigid container.

Seal, label and freeze.

To thaw: leave in wrappings in the refrigerator overnight.

Makes enough for 6 servings.

Variation

Rum butter

Make as for Brandy Butter above, substituting orange rind and juice and rum for the lemon and brandy.

Mincemeat

2 cups medium or dry cider
1 lb dark brown sugar
4 lb cooking apples
1 teaspoon ground allspice
1 teaspoon ground cinnamon
1 lb currants
1 lb seedless raisins
¼ lb glacé cherries, finely chopped
1 cup blanched almonds, finely chopped
Finely grated rind and juice of 1 lemon
1 miniature bottle brandy or rum

Cooking Time: 30–40 minutes.

This is an unusual mincemeat recipe using a fairly high proportion of cooking apples, and no suet. The mincemeat itself is boiled before packing into jars and storing – this makes it keep well. Make it in the autumn when cooking apples are plentiful, then store it in a cool dry place until Christmas.

Put the cider and sugar in a large saucepan and heat gently until the sugar has dissolved.

Meanwhile, peel, core and chop the apples and add to the pan. Stir in the remaining ingredients, except the brandy or rum, and bring slowly to the boil, stirring constantly. Lower the heat, half cover with a lid and simmer for approximately 30 minutes or until the mincemeat has become a soft pulp, stirring occasionally. Turn off the heat and leave mincemeat until quite cold. Stir in the brandy or rum, making sure that it is evenly distributed. Spoon the mincemeat into clean, dry jars with screw-topped lids, covering the top of mincemeat with a circle of wax paper before putting on lids.

Makes about 8 pounds.

Mincemeat flan

For the pastry:
1¾ cups flour
Pinch of salt
¼ lb (1 stick) butter or margarine
2 tablespoons sugar
1 egg yolk
2 tablespoons cold water

For the filling:
6 dessert apples
4 tablespoons butter
½ cup brown sugar
Finely grated rind and juice of 1 lemon
10 oz mincemeat

For the topping:
3 egg whites
¾ cup sugar

Cooking Time: 50 minutes.
Oven: 375°F, then reduce to 275°F.

To save time during the Christmas holiday, you may freeze this flan before adding the meringue topping. To serve, thaw the flan, coat in the meringue and bake.

Sift the flour and salt into a bowl. Add the butter or margarine in pieces and rub into the flour until the mixture resembles fine breadcrumbs. Stir in the sugar and egg yolk, then stir in the water and draw the dough together to form a smooth ball. Wrap in foil and chill in the refrigerator for 30 minutes. Roll out the dough on a lightly floured board to a circle large enough to line a 9 inch flan tin or flan ring placed on a baking sheet. Prick the base of the dough with a fork and chill in the refrigerator for another 30 minutes. Line the dough with foil and dry beans and bake blind in a fairly hot oven for 15 minutes. Remove foil and beans, return to the oven and bake for another 5 minutes until the pastry is golden. Remove the flan ring if used.

Peel apples, core with an apple corer and slice into thin rings. Melt the butter in a pan, add the apple rings, brown sugar, lemon rind and juice and cook gently for a few minutes until the apples are coated in the mixture. Cool. Arrange half the apple rings in the bottom of the pastry case, spoon in the mincemeat and top with the remaining apples.

Beat the egg whites until stiff, then beat in 1 tablespoon of the sugar. Fold in the remaining sugar, reserving 1 tablespoon for dusting. Pipe the meringue on top of the flan to cover the filling completely. Dust with the reserved sugar and bake in a very cool oven for 30 minutes until the meringue is golden. Remove from the oven and leave to rest for approximately 15 minutes before serving.

Cuts into 12 wedges.

Mincemeat flan; Mincemeat; Plum pudding

Plum pudding

½ lb pitted prunes, soaked overnight in
cold water, drained and finely chopped
½ lb golden raisins
1 lb dark raisins
½ lb currants
½ lb carrots, peeled and grated
1½ cups shredded beef suet
1 lb fresh white breadcrumbs (about 6
cups)
1¾ cups self-rising flour
1 cup sugar
¼ teaspoon salt
½ teaspoon baking powder
½ teaspoon ground allspice
½ teaspoon grated nutmeg
Finely grated rind and juice of 1 lemon
3 eggs, beaten
1¼ cups stout or ale
Milk to mix
Flour for sealing

Cooking Time: 6 hours.

This is a very old recipe for a traditional, rich Christmas pudding,
and it is one that improves in flavor the longer it is kept. If you like,
you can continue the old custom of burying a silver coin in the
pudding before steaming – but wrap it in foil first.

Put the dried fruit, carrots, suet, breadcrumbs, self-rising flour
and sugar in a large mixing bowl and stir well to mix. Add the
remaining dry ingredients and stir to combine. Stir in the lemon
rind and juice, eggs and stout and continue stirring until all the
ingredients are thoroughly combined, adding enough milk to make
a soft dropping consistency.

Spoon the mixture into greased pudding basins to come within
1 inch of each rim, packing the mixture down well with the back of a
spoon. Cover the top of each with a circle of greased wax paper. Put
a thick layer of flour on top of the wax paper, pressing it down well
with the back of a spoon, then cover with another circle of paper.
Cover the basins with a pudding cloth, muslin or aluminium foil,
leaving room for the puddings to rise during cooking. Tie securely.
Place the puddings in the top of a steamer or double boiler, or in a
large pan of gently bubbling water, and steam for at least six hours,
topping up the water level from time to time during cooking.

Remove puddings from the pan and leave until cold. Check that
the puddings are tightly sealed – the flour will have become a solid
paste – and renew the top piece of wax paper and the cloth if
necessary. Store in a cool dry place. Steam again for 2 to 3 hours
before serving.

Makes about 5 1 pound puddings.

Rum truffles

4 oz semi-sweet chocolate, broken into pieces
3 tablespoons rum
$\frac{1}{4}$ lb stale fruit cake
$\frac{3}{4}$ cup ground almonds
$\frac{1}{3}$ cup plus 2 teaspoons confectioners' sugar, sifted
2 tablespoons apricot jam, strained
2 tablespoons cocoa powder
1 cup chocolate sprinkles

Truffles make pretty presents if packaged in a festive-looking box, or they can be handed round with the coffee and liqueurs after Christmas dinner.

Put the chocolate and rum in a heatproof bowl and stand over a pan of gently simmering water. Heat until the chocolate melts, stirring occasionally.

Meanwhile, crumble the cake and ground almonds together in a bowl with the fingertips. Pour in the melted chocolate and the confectioners' sugar and stir well to combine. Turn out onto a board sprinkled with confectioners' sugar and knead lightly until smooth.

Shape the mixture into approximately 25 balls and brush with the jam. Put the cocoa and sprinkles together in a bowl and shake to combine. Add the truffles one at a time and shake the bowl until each truffle is evenly coated. Chill in the refrigerator until firm, then pack in cases.

To freeze: open freeze until solid, then pack carefully in a single layer in a rigid container. Seal, label and return to freezer.

To thaw: put frozen truffles in cases and thaw for approximately 1 hour at room temperature.

Makes about 25.

Rum truffles

Christmas cake

The basic design for this cake is simple, yet effective. Make the cake in three easy stages, starting it during the month of November, then there will be very little to do during the days immediately before Christmas. Follow the instructions for the Anniversary Cake (page 26), baking the rich fruit mixture in a 10 inch round cake pan. Leave to mature for one month, spooning over more spirits from time to time, if wished. Coat with the same quantity of almond paste as the Anniversary Cake, then leave to dry out for one week.

To decorate the cake:

1. Make up the same quantity of royal icing as for the Anniversary Cake (without food coloring) and use to coat the cake. Quickly scoop up the surplus icing, put in a bowl and cover with a lid or damp cloth. Leave cake and surplus icing overnight.
2. The next day, lift the cake onto a 12 inch round silver cake board. Thicken the surplus icing with the remaining confectioners' sugar as for the Anniversary Cake. Fit a pastry bag with a No. 8 star tube, put in some of the icing and pipe a large shell edge around the base of the cake to neaten it and join it to the board.
3. Fit a pastry bag with a No. 2 plain tube, put in some of the icing and pipe a diagonal line across the cake $\frac{1}{2}$ inch from the center. Pipe five lines parallel to this line $\frac{1}{4}$ inch apart. Repeat these five lines at right angles on the outer side of the cake, then overpipe each line on both sides. Neaten the ends of the lines by piping a small beading.
4. Using the No. 2 plain tube, pipe the words "Merry Christmas" in the large triangle formed by the lines. In the three remaining triangles pipe outlines of holly leaves and small circles for berries.
5. Put 3 tablespoons of the remaining icing in a separate bowl and thin it down with a little water to a running consistency. Color it with a few drops of green food coloring. Make a plain wax paper cone, put in the green icing and cut the end of the cone. Use to fill in the holly shapes.
6. Color the remaining icing with a few drops of bright red food coloring and put into a pastry bag fitted with a No. 2 plain tube. Overpipe the lines on the top of the cake and the lettering. Fill in the circles to represent holly berries. Pipe a looped line over the shell edging at the base of the cake.
7. Leave the icing to dry, then tie a red ribbon or cake frill around the cake.

Christmas cake

January 25th, the birthday of the Scottish poet Robert Burns,
is Burns' Night in Great Britain – one of the nights in the year when it is
customary to eat haggis. A traditional haggis contains the ground
lungs, liver and heart of a sheep, together with beef suet, onions,
oatmeal, gravy and plenty of seasoning. This mixture is put into a
sheep's stomach or paunch and boiled for several hours, then
served with Mashed "Nips" (turnips) and a glass or two of whisky.

Haggis pudding

For the suet pastry:
$1\frac{3}{4}$ cups self-rising flour
1 teaspoon salt
$\frac{2}{3}$ cup shredded beef suet
Scant $\frac{2}{3}$ cup water

For the filling:
2 tablespoons cooking oil
2 medium-sized onions, peeled and finely
chopped
$\frac{1}{2}$ lb lamb's liver, sliced
$\frac{1}{2}$ lb boned shoulder of mutton or lamb,
ground
2 oz can anchovies, soaked in milk for 30
minutes
$1\frac{1}{2}$ cups medium oatmeal
$\frac{2}{3}$ cup shredded beef suet
2 tablespoons finely chopped parsley
Finely grated rind and juice of 1 lemon
Salt and freshly ground black pepper
About $\frac{1}{4}$ cup red wine or beef stock

Cooking Time: $2\frac{3}{4}$ hours.

To make a traditional haggis it is necessary to have a sheep's pluck (lungs, liver and heart) and stomach bag, both of which are difficult to obtain. This is an adaption of the traditional haggis, and is steamed in a pudding basin. It should be served with plenty of rich brown gravy, mashed "nips" and baked potatoes.

To make the pastry: sift the flour and salt into a mixing bowl. Stir in the shredded suet. Mix in the water gradually to form a smooth elastic dough that leaves the sides of the bowl. Turn out onto a floured board, knead lightly, then roll into a circle large enough to line the inside of a $1\frac{1}{2}$ quart pudding basin. Cut out one quarter of the circle for the lid and reserve. Grease the inside of the basin and fit in the pastry lining, joining the edges in the basin with water. Set aside.

To make the filling: heat the oil in a pan, add the onions and fry gently until soft and lightly colored. Transfer to a mixing bowl and add the liver to the pan, with more oil if necessary. Fry the liver briskly until browned on all sides, then remove from the pan and set aside to cool. Add the lamb to the pan and fry until browned, stirring constantly. Put in the mixing bowl with the onion.

Drain the anchovies and grind with the liver until fine, then mix into the lamb and onion mixture with the oatmeal and beef suet. Stir in the parsley, lemon rind and juice, and plenty of salt and pepper. Add the red wine or stock gradually until the mixture is soft but not wet.

Spoon the haggis into the pastry-lined pudding basin. Roll out the reserved pastry for the lid and place on top of the haggis. Tuck in the edges and seal with a little water. Cover with a circle of foil with a pleat in the center. Tie securely with string. Place in the top of a steamer or double boiler, or in a large pan of gently bubbling water, and steam for $2\frac{1}{2}$ hours. Remove from the pan, leave to rest 5 minutes, then remove coverings and turn haggis out onto a warmed serving platter; or serve straight from the pudding basin. Serve immediately.
Serves 6–8.

Haggis pudding; Mashed "nips"

Mashed "nips"

About 3–3½ lb turnips or rutabagas,
peeled and diced
Salt
4 tablespoons butter
¼ cup light cream
1 teaspoon ground ginger
Freshly ground black pepper

Cooking Time: 30 minutes.

In Scotland, turnips and rutabagas are very popular winter vegetables, as well as being the traditional accompaniment to haggis on Burns' Night.

Cook the turnips or rutabagas in boiling salted water for approximately 25 minutes or until quite tender. Drain, then mash thoroughly with a potato masher or purée in an electric blender. Stir or work in the butter, then pour in the cream with the ginger, and salt and pepper to taste. Return to the rinsed-out pan and reheat gently. Transfer to a hot serving dish and serve.
Serves 6.

Shrove Tuesday precedes the first day of Lent
and the story goes that crêpes were made on
this day because housewives were anxious to use up all the eggs and
butter in the house before Lent. Nowadays, few people abstain from
eating these foods during Lent, but the custom of eating crêpes
on Shrove Tuesday still survives.

Crêpes

¾ *cup flour*
½ *teaspoon salt*
1 egg, beaten
1¼ *cups milk*
2 tablespoons cooking oil

To serve:
Superfine sugar for sprinkling
3 lemons, quartered

Cooking Time: 15 minutes.

The secret of making good crepes lies in having a good quality, heavy-based pan for frying, and it is a good idea to keep one pan specially for cooking crêpes. The oil should be very hot, and a very small amount of batter should be used for each crêpe so they are paper thin. Sift the flour and salt into a mixing bowl. Make a well in the center and put in the egg. Gradually add half the milk, beating in the flour vigorously until a thick batter is formed. Pour in the remaining milk and 1 teaspoon of the oil and beat until quite smooth.

Heat a little of the remaining oil in a 7 inch crêpe or frying pan and, when very hot, pour in approximately 2 tablespoons batter. Tilt the pan quickly so that the batter runs over the bottom of the pan. Cook over high heat until the underneath is golden brown. Toss the crêpe or turn over with a metal spatula, and cook on the other side until golden brown. Slide the crêpe out onto a hot plate, cover with another plate and keep warm in the oven while cooking the remaining crêpes in the same way.

To serve sprinkle each crêpe with sugar to taste, roll up, arrange on a warmed serving platter and sprinkle with a little more sugar. Place the lemon quarters around the edge of the platter.

To freeze: interleave crêpes with freezer paper or foil, then wrap stack of crêpes in foil or a freeze bag. Seal, label and freeze.

To thaw: unwrap and leave at room temperature for approximately 20 minutes, then reheat.

Makes 10–12.

Crêpes; Savory crêpes

Savory crêpes

For the filling:
2 tablespoons cooking oil
1 large onion, peeled and finely chopped
¾ lb ground beef
2 oz can anchovies, drained and soaked in milk for 30 minutes
1 teaspoon dill powder
2 tablespoons tomato paste
1¼ cups sour cream
About ½ cup beef stock to moisten
Freshly ground black pepper
2½ cups crêpe batter (see left)

Cooking Time: 30 to 40 minutes.

Heat the oil in a pan, add the onion and cook gently for approximately 5 minutes until soft and lightly colored. Add the ground beef and cook until browned, stirring occasionally.
Drain the anchovies and pound to a paste with a pestle and mortar. Add to the pan with the dill, tomato paste and 2 tablespoons sour cream. Stir well to combine and add enough stock to moisten. Season with plenty of pepper, then cook very gently for 20 minutes, stirring occasionally. Taste and adjust seasoning. Meanwhile, make the crêpes, using twice as much batter for each crêpe as called for in the recipe for crêpes (*left*). Keep each crêpe warm while making the remainder. When all the crêpes are made, lay each one flat on a board, put a few spoonfuls of filling on each, then roll up and place on a warmed serving platter. Keep warm while filling and rolling the remainder.
Heat the remaining sour cream, pour over the crêpes and serve immediately.
To freeze: pack in a single layer in a foil container without sour cream topping. Cover, seal, label and freeze.
To thaw: reheat crêpes from frozen in foil container in a moderate oven (350°F) for 35 minutes until heated through. Cover with sour cream before serving as above.
Serves 4.

All Hallow's Eve, as Halloween should be called, takes place on the last day of October, and is a time when old superstitions are revived and supernatural forces are believed to be about. The celebration of Halloween dates back to the times of the Druids who held their fire festival on this day. These days, Halloween is reserved for playing such games as ducking for apples and burning the nuts, for making lanterns out of pumpkins – and eating baked potatoes around an open fire.
In Great Britain, Guy Fawkes' Night follows Halloween on November 5th and up and down the country bonfires are lit to celebrate the disastrous Gunpowder Plot of 1605. Parkin is traditionally eaten around the bonfire and hot spiced drinks are passed round to warm the revellers on a cold November night.

Cheesy sausage rolls

1¾ cups flour
Pinch of salt
Pinch of cayenne
¼ lb (1 stick) butter or margarine
½ cup finely grated Cheddar cheese
1 egg yolk, beaten
Pinch each basil, parsley and oregano
½ lb pork sausage meat
A little milk to glaze

Cooking Time: 25–30 minutes.
Oven: 400°F, then reduce to 350°F.

Cheese-flavored shortcrust pastry gives sausage rolls added interest. The pastry is very rich, therefore make individual rolls as small as possible.
Sift the flour, salt and cayenne into a bowl. Add the butter or margarine in pieces and rub together with the fingertips until the mixture resembles fine breadcrumbs. Stir in the grated cheese and egg yolk and draw the mixture together with the fingertips to form a smooth dough. Form into a ball, wrap in foil and chill in the refrigerator for at least 30 minutes. Divide the dough in two and roll each piece out on a lightly floured board to an oblong shape approximately 4 inches wide.
Mix the dried herbs into the sausage meat, divide in two and roll with floured hands into long sausage shapes. Place the sausage meat on the dough and fold over to enclose. Brush the edges with a little milk and press firmly to seal. Brush all over the dough with milk, then cut into 1 to 2 inch lengths.
Place the sausage rolls on a baking sheet and bake just above the center of a fairly hot oven for 15 minutes. Reduce the heat to moderate and continue baking for another 10 to 15 minutes until the pastry is golden brown and crisp. Remove from the oven, transfer to a warmed serving platter and serve warm.
Makes about 15–20.

Cheesy sausage rolls; Fruity parkin

Fruity parkin

6 tablespoons butter or margarine
⅔ cup dark brown sugar
½ cup golden or light corn syrup
¼ cup black treacle
Finely grated rind and juice of 1 lemon
1⅓ cups self-rising flour
Pinch of salt
2 teaspoons ground ginger
2 cups medium oatmeal
4 dried apricots, soaked overnight drained
and finely chopped
½ cup golden raisins
½ cup chopped dates
About 6 tablespoons milk

Cooking Time: 45 minutes.
Oven: 350°F.

Always store parkin in an airtight tin for at least three days before cutting and eating. The parkin will become more moist the longer it is kept.

Put the butter or margarine, sugar, syrup and treacle in a saucepan and heat gently until dissolved, stirring occasionally. Remove from the heat and stir in the lemon rind and juice.

Sift the flour, salt and ginger into a bowl, then stir in the oatmeal and dried fruit. Stir in the melted mixture, then enough milk to make a soft dropping consistency. Beat well to combine. Grease a 9 × 5½ × 2 inch baking tin and line the base with greased wax paper. Pour in the parkin and bake in a moderate oven for approximately 45 minutes until firm to the touch. Remove from the oven, leave to cool in the tin for a few minutes, then turn out onto a wire rack. Leave until completely cold, then peel off the paper and store in an airtight tin.

Cuts into about 12 pieces.

Bonfire toffee

¼ lb (1 stick) butter
1⅓ cups brown sugar
¾ cup golden or light corn syrup
Walnut halves

Cooking Time: 15–20 minutes.

Use the largest saucepan available for making toffee as this will help prevent the toffee boiling over and sticking to the top of the cooker.
Brush a large shallow tin with a little of the butter and set aside. Put the remaining butter in a saucepan and heat gently until melted. Add the sugar and syrup and heat gently until the sugar has dissolved, stirring occasionally. Increase the heat and boil the mixture rapidly for approximately 10 minutes until the temperature reaches 310°F on a sugar thermometer. Remove from the heat and pour into the prepared tin. Leave to cool for 10 to 15 minutes, then mark into squares and put a walnut half in the middle of each. Leave until completely cold, then remove the squares of toffee from the tin and store in an airtight container. Makes about 1 lb.

Bonfire toffee; Toffee apples

Toffee apples

10 dessert apples, washed and dried
10 wooden sticks

For the toffee:
2 cups brown sugar
4 tablespoons butter
½ cup golden or light corn syrup
1 teaspoon lemon juice
⅔ cup water

Cooking Time: about 20 minutes.

Remove the stalks from the apples and push a wooden stick into each one.
Put all the ingredients for the toffee into a heavy-based saucepan and heat gently until dissolved, stirring occasionally. Increase the heat and boil rapidly, without stirring, until the toffee reaches a temperature of 290°F on a sugar thermometer. Remove from the heat.
Carefully dip the apples in the toffee one at a time. Make sure that they are completely covered in the toffee, then plunge into a bowl of cold water. Stand on well-oiled wax paper until set.
Makes 10.

In November both the Americans and Canadians
celebrate Thanksgiving Day. All over North America
housewives prepare celebration dinners of roast turkey with all the
trimmings: stuffing, cranberry sauce, roast or glazed sweet potatoes
and buttered Brussels sprouts. The traditional dessert for
Thanksgiving Day is Pumpkin Pie, made of
puréed pumpkin, sugar, eggs and spices in a pie case. The menu
given here is a traditional Thanksgiving one, but the recipe for
roast turkey can obviously be used for Christmas Day.

Roast turkey with stuffings

*1 oven-ready turkey (about 10–12 lb),
with the giblets*
4 tablespoons butter, softened
Salt and freshly ground black pepper

For the sausage meat and herb stuffing:
1 tablespoon butter
1 large onion, peeled and finely chopped
½ lb pork sausage meat
2 cups fresh white breadcrumbs
*2 teaspoons dried thyme, crumbled bay
leaf and basil*
1 tablespoon finely chopped parsley
1 egg, beaten
Salt and freshly ground black pepper

For the bacon and corn stuffing:
1 tablespoon butter
1 large onion, peeled and finely chopped
½ lb slab bacon, rind removed and chopped
10 oz package frozen corn
Salt
⅓ cup shredded beef suet
2 cups fresh white breadcrumbs
1 egg, beaten
Freshly ground black pepper

Cooking Time: 3¾–4 hours.
Oven: 325°F.

If only one stuffing is liked, then double the quantity given here
and use in both neck and body cavities. Any leftover mixture can
be formed into small balls, rolled in flour and fried until crisp, then
arranged around the bird on the serving platter.

Wash the turkey inside and out and dry thoroughly. Spoon the
prepared stuffings into the bird – sausage meat and herb in the
body cavity, bacon and corn in the neck end. Sew both openings
with trussing string and secure with skewers if necessary. Brush all
over the turkey with softened butter and sprinkle liberally with salt
and pepper. Cover with greased wax paper or foil and place on a
rack in a roasting pan. Roast in a warm oven for 3¾ to 4 hours,
basting and turning occasionally. Remove the paper or foil 15
minutes before the end of cooking time if a crisp brown skin is
liked. To test if done: pierce the thickest part of the thigh with a
skewer – the juices should run clear, not pink. Transfer the turkey
to a warmed serving platter and remove strings, and skewers if
used. Serve with gravy made from the giblets and cooking juices
from the bird, baked or roast potatoes, sausages and a selection of
seasonal vegetables.

To make the sausage meat and herb stuffing: melt butter in a pan,
add the onion and cook gently until soft and lightly colored.
Transfer to a bowl, stir in the remaining stuffing ingredients with
plenty of salt and pepper and mix thoroughly.

To make the bacon and corn stuffing: melt butter in a pan, add the
onion and cook gently until soft and lightly colored. Remove the
onion from the pan with a slotted spoon and put in a bowl. Add the
bacon to the pan, cook until crisp and golden, then transfer to the
bowl. Cook the corn in boiling salted water for 5 minutes, then
drain and add to the bowl with the remaining stuffing ingredients.
Season to taste with salt and pepper and mix thoroughly.

Serves 10–12.

Pumpkin pie

For the pastry:
1¾ cups flour
Pinch of salt
4 tablespoons butter or margarine
4 tablespoons lard
2 tablespoons sugar
Finely grated rind of 1 lemon
1–2 tablespoons cold water

For the filling:
16 oz can unseasoned pumpkin purée
1 small can evaporated milk (equivalent to 2 cups)
2 tablespoons honey
⅔ cup brown sugar
Juice of 1 lemon
1 teaspoon ground ginger
1 teaspoon ground cinnamon
½ teaspoon grated nutmeg
Pinch of salt
2 eggs, beaten

Cooking Time: 45 minutes.
Oven: 375°F.

Although this pie can be made with fresh pumpkin, it is often difficult to obtain – and time-consuming to cook and purée. Cans of unseasoned pumpkin purée are stocked all year round at good grocers and delicatessens. Sift the flour and salt into a bowl. Add the butter or margarine and lard in pieces and rub into the flour with the fingertips until the mixture resembles fine breadcrumbs. Stir in the sugar and lemon rind and enough cold water to bind the mixture together. Form into a ball, wrap in foil and chill in the refrigerator for at least 30 minutes.
Roll out the dough on a lightly floured board and use to line a 9½ inch fluted flan tin with removable base. Reserve the leftover pieces of dough for the lattice. Place on a baking sheet, prick the base, then chill in the refrigerator for another 30 minutes. Meanwhile, make the filling: put all the filling ingredients in a bowl and stir well to combine. Pour into the flan case. Roll out the reserved pieces of dough and cut into strips to form a lattice on top of the filling. Seal with a little water. Bake in a fairly hot oven for 45 minutes or until the filling is set and the pastry golden. Remove from the oven and leave to cool. Before serving, remove from the flan tin, and place on a serving platter. Serve with plenty of whipped heavy cream.
To freeze: open freeze cooled pumpkin pie until solid, then wrap loosely in foil and overwrap in a freezer bag. Seal, label and return to freezer.
To thaw: unwrap and leave at room temperature for 3 hours.
Serves 6–8.

Index